T0028745

Praise for
Goliath Must Fall for Young Readers

The story of David and Goliath has always intrigued me. It's a story you can read over and over again and pick up a different message each time. I've looked up to Louie for a long time, so when I heard he was writing a book on defeating the giants in your life, I couldn't wait to hear his perspective. I had a major giant in my life called fear. If you are battling that same giant, then the young readers edition of *Goliath Must Fall* is a must read.

> Sadie Robertson, author, speaker, actor,
> and founder of Live Original

Louie has taken the life-changing message that spoke to adults so profoundly in *Goliath Must Fall* and adapted it seamlessly for younger readers. He walks young minds toward the road to redemption through godly wisdom and relatable transparency. He doesn't just help them conquer the Goliaths in their lives; he shares his own. This book offers freedom for any kid who is ready to see their giants defeated.

> Lecrae, Grammy Award–winning artist,
> songwriter, and producer

The young readers edition of *Goliath Must Fall* will ignite your desire to see your giants defeated and step into all God has for you.

> Christine Caine, founder of A21 and Propel Women

God has created us for His purpose and joy, but often the choices we make rob us of the freedom found in relationship with Him and in community. Louie Giglio identifies the giants in our lives that can stifle us and gently invites us to listen to the voice of the Shepherd, who "sets our hearts free."

> Ravi Zacharias, author and speaker

GOLIATH
MUST
FALL

for Young Readers

GOLIATH
MUST
FALL

Winning the Battle Against Your Giants

For Young Readers

LOUIE GIGLIO

WITH TAMA FORTNER

Goliath Must Fall for Young Readers

© 2020 Louie Giglio

Tommy Nelson, PO Box 141000, Nashville, TN 37214

All rights reserved. No portion of this book may be reproduced, stored in a retrieval system, or transmitted in any form or by any means—electronic, mechanical, photocopy, recording, scanning, or other—except for brief quotations in critical reviews or articles, without the prior written permission of the publisher.

Published in Nashville, Tennessee, by Tommy Nelson. Tommy Nelson is an imprint of Thomas Nelson. Thomas Nelson is a registered trademark of HarperCollins Christian Publishing, Inc.

The Writer is represented by Cyle Young of C.Y.L.E. (Cyle Young Literary Elite, LLC), a literary agency.

Tommy Nelson titles may be purchased in bulk for educational, business, fund-raising, or sales promotional use. For information, please e-mail SpecialMarkets@ThomasNelson.com.

Unless otherwise noted, Scripture quotations are taken from the Holy Bible, New International Version®, NIV®. Copyright © 1973, 1978, 1984, 2011 by Biblica, Inc.® Used by permission of Zondervan. All rights reserved worldwide. www.zondervan.com. The "NIV" and "New International Version" are trademarks registered in the United States Patent and Trademark Office by Biblica, Inc.® Scripture quotations marked CEV are taken from the Contemporary English Version. Copyright © 1991, 1992, 1995 by American Bible Society. Used by permission. Scripture quotations marked ICB are taken from the International Children's Bible®. Copyright © 1986, 1988, 1999, 2015 by Thomas Nelson. Used by permission. All rights reserved. Scripture quotations marked NKJV are taken from the New King James Version®. © 1982 by Thomas Nelson. Used by permission. All rights reserved. Scripture quotations marked NLT are taken from the Holy Bible, New Living Translation. © 1996, 2004, 2007, 2013 by Tyndale House Foundation. Used by permission of Tyndale House Ministries, Carol Stream, Illinois 60188. All rights reserved. Scripture quotations marked TLB are taken from The Living Bible. Copyright © 1971. Used by permission of Tyndale House Publishers, a Division of Tyndale House Ministries, Carol Stream, Illinois 60188. All rights reserved.

ISBN 978-1-4002-2368-8 (audiobook)
ISBN 978-1-4002-2366-4 (eBook)
ISBN 978-1-4002-2363-3 (HC)
ISBN 978-1-4002-5096-7 (TP)

Library of Congress Cataloging-in-Publication Data

Names: Giglio, Louie, author. | Fortner, Tama, 1969- author.
Title: Goliath must fall for young readers : winning the battle against your giants / Louie Giglio with Tama Fortner.
Description: Nashville, Tennessee : Thomas Nelson, 2020. | Audience: Ages 8-12 | Summary: "Goliath Must Fall for Young Readers by Louie Giglio helps kids and preteens learn that God is present, God is powerful, and He alone can conquer the giants in their lives"-- Provided by publisher.
Identifiers: LCCN 2020019293 (print) | LCCN 2020019294 (ebook) | ISBN 9781400223633 (hardcover) | ISBN 9781400223664 (epub)
Subjects: LCSH: David, King of Israel--Juvenile literature. | Goliath (Biblical giant)--Juvenile literature. | Children--Religious life--Juvenile literature.
Classification: LCC BS580.D3 G58 2020 (print) | LCC BS580.D3 (ebook) | DDC 222/.4309505--dc23
LC record available at https://lccn.loc.gov/2020019293
LC ebook record available at https://lccn.loc.gov/2020019294

Written by Louie Giglio with Tama Fortner.

Contents

The Story Begins:
The Giant

The king ducked his head, shuffled out of his tent, and stared at the far hill on the other side of the valley, just outside his war camp. His breakfast rumbled on an uneasy stomach. All over the valley, the clank of cooking pots could be heard as men lit fires and munched on bread and cheese. It wouldn't be long until the shouter's voice came again. The king let out a deep sigh.

"How many days does this make?" he asked his aide.

"Forty, sir," the aide answered. He knew King Saul already knew the number. But the aide's life depended on giving the correct answer to the king.

"Can you see him coming?" the king asked.

The aide squinted, lifted a hand to shade his brow, and nodded. "Right on time, sir."

The king grumbled as he slipped into his royal robes, then he went silent. His shoulders slumped.

"You!" boomed a shout from across the valley. "Why don't you line up for battle today, or are you too afraid?"

All the soldiers in the Israelite camp turned to watch, many trembling. The taunt was nothing new, but the soldiers took no action. There were no orders. No volunteers. They hated the one who stood in front of them, but none of them was brave enough to try and stop him. So they stood and watched and listened.

TAUNT: to mock, insult, jeer, sneer, or torment

The shouter was a beast of a man. Hairy, ugly, loud, and rude. He was scarred from a hundred previous battles. A bronze helmet rested on his head. A massive coat of scale armor covered his body. Bronze plates protected his legs. The shouter gripped a massive spear in one hand, and a smaller bronze spear was slung across his back. His shield bearer stood before him, grinning as he looked forward to a fight. With all that armor on the brute, even the archers' arrows couldn't hurt him. And with an entire army behind the beast, the swordsmen couldn't rush him. The spearmen and chariot riders couldn't get close enough before they would be wiped out. The giant was undefeatable. And no one knew that better than the giant himself.

GOLIATH AND HIS ARMOR

Goliath truly was a giant of a man, standing roughly nine feet, nine inches tall. His battle coat was made of bronze and weighed 125 pounds. This was no ordinary coat, either. It was made from scale armor—overlapping pieces of bronze, much like a fish's scales. It was almost impossible for an arrow or sword to cut through such armor.

In addition to a massive sword, Goliath carried a long spear, or *javelin*. The head of it was made of iron and weighed fifteen pounds by itself. The shaft of the spear was as thick as a weaver's rod, or about two and a half inches around.

His shield was so large and heavy that another man—called a shield bearer—carried it into battle for him.

"You bunch of babies!" the giant shouted. "Am I not a Philistine, and are you not the servants of King Saul? Let's have a contest for men! I'll make you the same offer I gave you yesterday. You choose a man. We'll choose a man. The two men will fight. Whoever wins the battle wins the war. I'll be the man for our side. Who do you have on yours?" He laughed with a long, loud cackle.

The giant already knew the answer. No one was going to stand up to him.

The aide looked at King Saul. "Sir, do you have any answer for Goliath *today*?"

The king ignored the question. No, there was no answer *today*. There was no answer yesterday nor the day before that. The aide knew this. There had been no answer for the nearly six weeks since this whole mess started. There was no answer, because nobody in the Israelite army could defeat this giant. Everyone knew it. And no one knew it better than King Saul himself, one of the tallest, strongest, and most experienced warriors in the entire Israelite army.

DEFY: to challenge or dare

"So that's a *no*, then?" Goliath yelled. He spit on the ground and added, "You're worthless! The whole lot of you. Powerless. Weak. Just like your God. I defy you, and I defy your God. I'll wait until you're ready to fight like men. See you tomorrow, chumps." With that, Goliath and his shield bearer turned on their heels and stomped back to their camp.

King Saul turned to his aide and asked, "You've searched everywhere in camp for the strongest fighters, right? How much is the reward up to now?"

"Great wealth," the aide muttered. They went through the same checklist every day.

"Anything else?"

"No taxes for the soldier's family."

"Right. Have we forgotten anything?"

The aide cleared his throat. "Your daughter in marriage, sir. The soldiers all know she's part of the deal."

The king sighed again. He looked at the ground and said, "Carry on, then." He turned around and shuffled back inside his tent.

Defeated for one more day.

CONTEST OF CHAMPIONS

In Bible times, wars were sometimes decided by a contest between two men. Each side would choose one man—called a *champion*—to fight for them. The two champions would meet in the middle and fight to the death. The side whose champion won the contest then won the war.

THE GIANT *MUST* FALL

A lot of us face a giant every day. Okay, maybe not an actual giant named Goliath carrying a massive spear and shouting insults at us. But we're all facing some sort of huge, impossible challenge or problem that is messing up our lives. And we might not even know it. Maybe it's fear or worry. Maybe it's an addiction. (Yep, even a little one. We'll talk about this later.) Maybe it's anger. Maybe it's being rejected or feeling like you're never quite good enough. Or maybe it's the sneaky giant of comfort (I'll explain this guy later).

Have you ever felt the way King Saul and the Israelite army did? Like some kind of giant is standing in front of you, insulting you, and daring you to do something about it? You've tried everything you can think of to stop the giant, but you feel powerless. Stuck. You know you're young. These are supposed to be some of the best days of your life. But sometimes they're not. Because of this stupid giant. And you don't know what to do about it. If this sounds like your story, then this book is for you.

If someone asked if there's a giant in our lives, we'd probably answer with a quick no. You might think, *I don't have any Goliaths in my life. I'm good. I'm just doing my thing and living life.*

Some of you would say *yes*, though. You know you have a giant staring you down, and you're reading this book because you want to know how to defeat it.

The truth is, we all have some sort of giant in our

ARE YOU **READY** FOR YOUR GIANT TO FALL?

GIANT: anything that keeps you from being who God created you to be, such as fear, rejection, comfort, anger, or addiction

---

lives. It's always lurking nearby and stealing our joy.

It doesn't have to be a gigantic giant, like drugs, alcohol, an eating disorder, or depression. Giants come in all shapes and sizes. Some march right up to you like Goliath. Others sneak around and attack when you're not looking, like perfectionism, bullies, peer pressure, fear, anger, or worrying about your looks. The good news is it's not God's plan for you to live with *any* sort of giant in your life. God wants your giants to fall. God wants you to live free of giants. And you can!

No matter how big your giant is, God has a message for you today: *You. Can. Live. Free.*

I know, because I've been face-to-face with my own giants. And I've seen how God's power and strength will knock them down.

In this book I'm going to show you a new way to look at the story of David and Goliath. Through that story I'm going to show you how your own giant will fall. Because this isn't just about *wishing* that your giant will fall someday, sometime. No . . .

Goliath *must* fall.

It's time for you to say, "There's a giant in my life

that's holding me back, and it's got to go down. Now. Today. This giant isn't going to bother me anymore. It must stop talking to me, because God wants me to live free. God wants to get the glory of being the champion who knocks down my giant. That's why Goliath *must* fall."

Now, here's the part that can get a little confusing. It's really good news, though, so stick with me: The fact is, your giant *has already fallen.* You see, when Jesus died on the cross, He defeated all the

> NO MATTER HOW BIG YOUR GIANT IS, GOD HAS A MESSAGE FOR YOU TODAY: *YOU. CAN. LIVE. FREE.*

giants of the world. But look at *who* defeated the giants: *Jesus*, not you by yourself. You need Jesus' power working in your life to defeat your giants. How do you get that power? By following Him. It's the power of Christ in your life that knocks the giant down. This *must* happen for two main reasons:

1. *Your good.* God wants you to live free, not all tied up in knots of worry and fear.
2. *His glory.* God will get the glory when the world sees that He is bigger than your giants. And that will help the world learn to trust Him too.

Yes, you still have a responsibility in this giant-slaying process. You need to trust that God is bigger than your giants. If there's a voice in your head that says, *Nope. Your giant will taunt you forever. Your life will never change for the better*, then I want you to know that that voice isn't the voice of Jesus. It belongs to a giant that can—and will—be silenced!

Ever since Adam and Eve first chomped on the one fruit God said not to eat, sin has been a problem. And it's a problem for every single one of us. Sin builds a wall between us and God. Jesus came to earth and died on the cross to tear down that wall. Because of Him, we can be close to God again. And then Jesus rose from the grave so we could live with the power of His Spirit inside us—the same power that raised Him to life again.

You are closer than you think to a life free of giants. A life that shines with God's glory. Are you ready for your giant to fall?

—Pastor Louie

CHAPTER 1

Bigger Than Your Giant

Not long ago a woman was killed by her *pet* tiger. I'm not going to go into details, but it was bad. *Very* bad.

This whole event made me sad. But I also wondered, *Why would anyone have a pet tiger?* (No offense if you have a Bengal tiger in your backyard.)

Tigers are meat eaters! They survive in the wild by hunting and killing their prey. And a tiger will always be a tiger. Why would anyone try to make a pet out of one of these natural-born killers?

Here's what I think happened. When the woman first met the tiger, it was small and playful and cuddly. I bet she held that cub and it looked up at her in delight. A bond was formed. She gave her pet tiger cub a name.

Maybe Mooshie or BooBoo or Stripey or Elwood. She took it home and gave it a warm space to sleep and a safe place to play. All was well, day after day after day after day.

Until.

Elwood.

Grew.

Then that playful pet grew into what it truly was: a savage killer.

That's pretty much what happens with our giants— the bad habits we form, the wrong choices we make, the lies we believe, the same old broken ways of thinking that we don't let go of.

> OUR GIANTS ARE SHOWING THEIR TRUE COLORS—AND THEY AREN'T PETS ANYMORE. THEY'RE SAVAGE KILLERS.

They didn't start out as giants. If they had, we'd have never taken them home. No, these "pets" started out as cute and cuddly babies. They didn't look like they'd do us any harm. They were fun. They made us feel good. We formed bonds with these pets and gave them a warm place to stay in our minds and hearts and lives.

But these pets have grown. They're showing their true colors—and they aren't pets anymore. They're savage killers. Nine-foot-tall giants. They're ripping into us and tearing our lives apart.

We *really* want to get rid of these giants.

But how?

MY OWN PET GIANT

Goliath wasn't born nine feet tall. And whatever you're wrestling with wasn't born a giant either. I'm guessing it was actually fun or comforting in the beginning. Your *killer* was disguised as a friend you couldn't live without. Then one day—a day you didn't choose—the mask came off and the giant punched you in the throat.

I know what I'm talking about because I've been attacked by my own giant. It beat me up and pushed me into a deep, dark hole of depression and anxiety. Since then, I've figured out that anxiety is not my giant. It's just a symptom of my giant's attack on me.

So what was my giant? Looking back, I see the footprints of not one but two of my own Goliaths: control and rejection.

You see, wherever I am, I want to make things better. I see what *is*, but I dream of what *can be*. Whether I'm driving through a city, eating in a restaurant, or walking through a slum in Haiti, I'm constantly thinking of things I want to change for the better and how I can get people to help me change them. But that's a good thing, right?

The problem is that my dreaming talent can also invite the baby cub of control into the mix. Here's the deal: I want to change things for the better, which is great, but I also want to be in *control* of how it's done. Trying to control the world is a disaster waiting to happen. Why? Because we're never really in control.

ANXIETY: a feeling of doubt, dread, fear, nervousness, or worry that just won't seem to go away

Then there's the giant of rejection. If you add my need to be in control to my need to be liked by everyone, you have a perfect storm. I've been a pastor and speaker for many years now, and when I first started out, I spoke here, there, and everywhere. I was always on the move. So if people didn't like me in one place, it didn't matter. I'd soon be off to another group of people.

Then we started Passion City Church and planted ourselves in one place. I thought I could make everyone happy (*control* is talking now). And I really felt like I *needed* to make them happy. But I couldn't make everyone happy (no one can, by the way). When my giant need for control met and married my giant fear of rejection, they tag-teamed me like two pro wrestlers. They slammed me onto the mat and hurled me out of the ring. My "pets" of being in control and being liked had grown into full-fledged giants. They were taunting me and defying my God.

They were (and honestly, they still are sometimes) a couple of my giants.

What about you? What are your giants?

MEET THE GIANTS

Some of you know exactly what your giant is. You don't even need to think about it, because you battle it every day.

Others of you aren't exactly sure what to call your giant. It's not as easy to see. All you know is that something isn't right and you want to fix it.

So let's talk about some of the more common kinds of giants and how they can hurt us.

- **The Giant of Fear:** It's not like we walk around shaking in our boots all the time. But worry and anxiety are a big piece of who we are. They shake us up and rattle our world. They make us dread the nighttime because we stay up thinking about everything that scares us. Maybe we fear a person or something that might happen. Whatever it is, fear is ruling over us and holding us back from what God created us to do. And it keeps the brightness of God's glory from shining in our lives.

- **The Giant of Rejection:** We're afraid that if we don't get everything perfect, then people won't like us. If we ever take a break, if we ever turn in something less than perfect, if we ever say the wrong thing, if we ever show up in the wrong outfit, if we ever stop doing what everyone else wants us to do, then we're not going to get the approval we long for.

- **The Giant of Comfort:** Comfort isn't wrong if we're talking about resting or taking a break to get our strength and energy back. But comfort can become a huge problem if it keeps us from doing the hard things we need to do. If comfort is our giant, then we're taking the easiest path every time. We're doing just enough to get by. But the easiest path might not be the best path. It may not be healthy for our bodies, or it might not be the path that Jesus wants us to take because He has a special job for us to do.

- **The Giant of Anger:** It doesn't have to be throwing stuff and purple-faced screaming. Anger can simmer inside us, like water bubbling in a pot, until one day we can't keep a lid on our temper. We lash out for no good reason. We say something while we're mad, and we wish we could take it back. We know this anger is keeping us from God's best for us, but we just can't seem to get a handle on it.

- **The Giant of Addiction:** Lots of different addictions taunt us, and most of us struggle with at least one. We think addictions make us feel good, but they actually just put a mask over us so we don't think about the problem that's really bothering us. We usually think of addiction as big things, like drugs or alcohol or gambling. But it can be other things too. Like food, sugar, the internet, or video games. Or maybe it's the wrong kind of friend. A wrong kind of thought. Maybe we blame other people for our mistakes. We tell ourselves, *Well, this is just the way I am,* and some days we even believe that lie.

When a giant first steps on the scene, we might just put up with it. We might even think of reasons to keep it around. We think, *It's not really so bad, is it?* Or maybe we wrestle with it and wish it were gone. But it's hard, so we give up and end up letting it stick around anyway. Some days we still fight to get rid of the giant, but the problem never seems to go away completely.

How do we get rid of the giants? *Jesus.*

WHATEVER GIANT WE'RE BATTLING MIGHT BE BIG—BUT IT'S *NOT* BIGGER THAN JESUS.

Jesus said, "A thief comes to steal and kill and destroy. But I came to give life—life in all its fullness" (John 10:10 ICB). Jesus came to earth, died on the cross, and was raised up from the grave so that we could "really live" (1 Thessalonians 3:8). He wants to give us back what the giants are stealing from us—our freedom and His glory.

That starts with seeing and believing that whatever giant we're battling might be big—but it's *not* bigger than Jesus. Nine feet tall is nothing to Him.

We're going to see this in the story of David and Goliath. If you haven't heard this tale before, get ready. And if you have, there's a twist to the story I've just got to tell you about. It's a life-changing way of seeing Jesus *in* the story that changes everything about the way your giant is going down.

THE KID COMES TO DEATH VALLEY

In the story of David and Goliath, the ancient army of the Philistines was fighting against the army of Israel, the people of God. This happened a lot in the Old Testament. The Philistine army was a constant threat to God's people, and the two armies often clashed. The Philistines had their own god, a phony guy called Dagon. They were an evil people, and they hated all those who followed the one true God.

A lot of times the Philistines had the upper hand over the Israelites, and that was exactly what was happening when David walked onto the scene in 1 Samuel 17. Here's the story:

Picture a valley in ancient Israel. It's rocky and green and thorny. It's called the Valley of Elah, and through that valley flows the Brook of Elah. You'd think it would be a peaceful, inviting place, right? But it isn't. It's soon going to be the valley of death.

On each side of the brook is a hillside. The Philistine army was camped on one hillside, and the army of Israel was camped on the other. Every morning the armies would march out, look across the valley, and stare each other down.

When our story opens, the two armies weren't doing a lot of actual fighting. Instead, the army of Israel was being held back by a crude soldier named Goliath. He was a big, huge, giant Philistine, over nine feet tall, a champion fighter, a fierce and awesome-looking warrior with thick body armor.

Every day Goliath would come out and yell insults at

the army of Israel. He'd strut right down into the valley with his army behind him, glare up at the Israelites, and shout, "Cowards! You and your God are not big enough to take us on. I challenge you to a fight, and I defy your God! If anyone's brave enough to fight me, then come on down. Whoever wins the fight will win the whole war. All you gotta do is get past me." (That's not exactly what it says in 1 Samuel 17, but you get the idea.)

Day after day Goliath did this. A week passed. Two weeks. Three weeks. Four. Day after day, the insults continued. Day after day, not one of the Israelites dared to go down to fight. Goliath did this for *forty* days, but not a single soldier from the highly trained Israelite army dared to face Goliath alone.

The Israelite army was scared.

Discouraged.

Frozen.

Sunk.

A single giant had shut down the entire Israelite army. They'd lost the fight, and they hadn't even gone to battle yet.

Think for a moment about who the ancient Israelites were. Why were they so terrified? All they had to do was remember how God had miraculously rescued them from slavery in Egypt. He'd spilt the sea wide open for them. He'd guided them through the wilderness with a cloud by day and fire at night. When they were thirsty,

God made water appear. When they were hungry, God gave them manna to eat. He'd taken them across the Jordan River and brought them into the promised land. He'd sent the mighty walls of Jericho tumbling down with a shout of praise. Time and time again, God had done miraculous things for His people. They were His *chosen* people.

HELP WAS ON THE WAY.

But they'd forgotten.

Now, in fairness, we've got to give the Israelite army a bit of a break. I've never fought a nine-foot giant before, and I can't say that I'd have gone up against an armor-plated warrior standing three feet taller than me.

But what if he had threatened the people I love? There's a good chance I'd take a shot at a nine-foot giant then. Especially if I had a sword and some armor. Yet not a single one of the Israelites was willing to fight. One loud beast of a man was stopping the entire army of God. What a gloomy thought.

Fortunately, help was on the way. And it was coming from a surprising source.

On the fortieth day a kid named David came up to the Israelite camp. Most folks at the time didn't think David was anything special. The only person who'd ever thought much of him was an old prophet named Samuel, who'd come to the family's house once and anointed

David's head with oil. But that had been a while back. David was the youngest of a whole bunch of older brothers. If you have older brothers (or sisters), you probably know how this goes.

While the men in the family went off to do the fighting, young David's job was to stay home with his aging father and take care of the family sheep.

On that particular day when he came to camp, David was bringing supplies to his older brothers who were up on the front line. Basically, David was just a delivery boy.

The kid everybody yelled at to bring more cheese.

TRAINED FOR THE FIGHT

Just as David was saying hello to his brothers, Goliath strutted out and started yelling his daily insults. And in that moment something snapped inside David. I picture him doing a double take. He was like, "Wait a minute. What's this beast yelling at us?"

The voice of Goliath came clearer, and the giant yelled, "You idiots are actually putting your trust in the God of Israel? Your God is worthless. He's weak. He's nothing—just like you're nothing. Our god can smash your God."

David's eyes narrowed. His lips tightened. He asked his brothers, "Who is this joker? How is he getting away with saying all this about our God? Why is nobody taking him on?"

David's brothers stuttered, "Yeah, well, take a good look at this guy. His name is Goliath, and nobody wants to fight him. It's certain death. Just shut up and bring me another hunk of bread."

David glared across the valley.

"I'll fight him," he declared. "I'm going to shut him up."

What?

Imagine how David's announcement went over with David's brothers.

I mean, picture a boxing match. Who would you pick?

In the red corner, wearing nothing but sandals and a tunic, is a runt of a kid named David. No armor. No sword. No shield. No army training.

And in the other corner, wearing 125 pounds of steel-plated armor, is an experienced enemy warrior. He is taller than, well, everyone and is solid muscle from head to toe. Highly trained in all kinds of combat. Carries a spear. A sword. Huge helmet. He's got an armor bearer just to carry all his gear. He's got a full army at his back. Breathes fire. Crushes mere men.

Yeah, *that's* a fair fight.

David's brothers were like, "Kid, you're embarrassing

us. The Israelite army is filled with experienced fighters, and none of them is willing to take on Goliath. Now you want to fight him? You've lost your mind. Get lost before we tell Dad."

But David hadn't lost his mind, and he had some real-life training to fall back on. This wouldn't be his first fight. In all those years of tending sheep, David had actually been receiving a very advanced education. His trainer was none other than God Himself.

Part of David's training was writing songs about God, studying the facts and history of His people, and learning who God was and what He had done. Another part of David's training had been far less poetic and far more hands-on.

THESE VICTORIES HAPPENED THANKS TO THE POWER OF GOD.

One day a huge bear growled his way up to David's flock and grabbed one of the prized lambs. It was David's job to rescue the lamb. There was no help in sight. No one to call—and no phones anyway. So David went after the bear and rescued the sheep from its mouth. Now, this was no cute little cub. It was a massive, hungry monster of an animal. But when that bear turned on David, the shepherd boy seized it by its hair, struck it, and killed it.

And that wasn't David's only fight. Another afternoon a huge roaring lion came up to the flock and had the same idea. David took his shepherd's rod and beat the lion lifeless. David knew these victories happened thanks to the power of God.

Now, King Saul heard about David's offer and had him brought to his tent. David told his stories to Saul and gave glory to God for the results. David said, "Sir, I have killed lions and bears . . . and I can kill this worthless Philistine. He shouldn't have made fun of the army of the living God! The LORD has rescued me from the claws of lions and bears, and he will keep me safe from the hands of this Philistine" (1 Samuel 17:36–37 CEV).

Saul stood frozen for a moment.

"You killed a bear? *And* a lion?"

The king stared at the boy. He was small, but maybe . . .

"Nobody else wants to fight him," Saul said, "but you can have a turn if you're so sure about it all. But at least put on some armor first. Wait, you don't have any armor? Here—wear mine."

David put on the king's armor. It was shiny and solid, the best of the best. But David wasn't used to it and could hardly walk. "This isn't going to work for me," David said. "I need to take this off. God's got another plan."

David went down to the brook and chose five smooth stones. He put the stones in his shepherd's bag, took out his sling, and went out to face the giant.

GOD'S
POWER
AND
MIGHT
ARE
ALWAYS
GREATER
THAN
YOUR
GIANTS.

This fight didn't last long. If you'd paid a lot of money for a front-row seat, you'd have been disappointed. But the fight, though fast, was stunning.

Goliath and David swapped a few words. David took out one stone, slung it at the giant, and the giant fell at his feet, dead. *Bam.*

Ten seconds after the opening bell, everything was over.

ONE GIANT, TWO GIANTS, . . . A DOZEN?

Why is this story so important for us as Christians? Is it only so we can have a cool story to tell in Sunday school? Or is it because God wants us to know it's possible for huge giants to go down cold?

You might have a nine-foot-tall giant in your life, one that taunts and terrifies you day after day after day. But with the power of God, that giant will fall. It doesn't matter how big it is. God's power and might are always greater.

Or maybe you're battling a whole team of giants. There may be problems coming at you from every side. The same was true in the Bible. Did you know Goliath isn't the only giant in the Bible? He was from a whole line of oversized, evil warriors. Read 1 Chronicles 20.

There's Sippai and Lahmi and even a gargantuan fighter with six fingers on each hand and six toes on each foot.

God doesn't want us to be discouraged if we face more than one giant. He wants us to know that He's able to take them all down. And we'll soon see He already has. No giant is a match for Jesus. Every giant can—and will—fall.

Do we believe that?

Are we ready to be free of our giants?

> ## NO GIANT IS A MATCH FOR JESUS. EVERY GIANT CAN— AND WILL—FALL.

Jesus wants us to know that He is completely and totally able to take down the giants in our lives. It may look like that six-fingered, six-toed, furious, foaming, fearless giant coming at us just can't be beaten. But through the power of Jesus, that giant can—and will—fall down.

THE ULTRA-IMPORTANT TWIST TO THE STORY

In this book we're going to look at some of the most common, harmful giants—the ones that look huge and unbeatable. And we're going to see how these giants will fall. But I'm not going to just give you that tired old saying "You can do it if you try." Because you can't. Not alone. But you're going to meet a fighter who can do it for you.

That's where the big twist in this story comes in:

We are *not* David in the story of David and Goliath.

I know that's probably not what you heard at church. It's more likely that while the speaker was telling the story of David and Goliath, he or she said something like this: "David was a young person, and you're a young person too. David won, so now you can win too. David took up his sling. David choose his five smooth stones. David marched up the battlefield. David took down the giant. If you want to take down your giant, then you gotta be like David. Just get your sling. Choose your stones. And aim big!"

Everybody gets a little pumped up at a message like that. We think, *Okay. That's me. I can do this! I just need to have more courage. I just need to aim big. I can take down my giant with one shot.*

What happens? Maybe we do get extra brave for a little while. Maybe we try harder and really go after our giant of a problem. But it's kind of like watching an avenger movie and then feeling like we have superhuman power. You might stand in your living room and act out scenes from the movie. You might imagine you're flying through the air, hurling balls of fire at the bad guys. But it's just an act, right? After we get fired up about the lesson at church, it's not long before we go back to living with our bigger-than-ever giant. Those chants and cheers of "You can do it" or "Dare to be a David" just don't work, and our giant stays put.

Here's why: we are *not* David in this story. You know who David is in our story?

Jesus.

Jesus is David in the story of David and Goliath. Jesus kills the giant. Jesus fights the battles for us. Jesus stares down the face of impossible problems. Jesus takes up His sling. Jesus chooses the five smooth stones. Jesus takes aim at the giant. The giant falls because of the work of Jesus.

Sure, we have to do our part. We have to keep talking to God every day through prayer and learning His Word. But we can't take down these giants on our own. We need the power of Jesus.

I know what you might be thinking: *Are you telling me we've had this story wrong the whole time?*

Not exactly. I just think we haven't been seeing the *whole* story. We can and *should* take courage from David. But the Bible isn't about what we can do for ourselves. The entire Bible points to Jesus as the Savior of

JESUS
FIGHTS
THE
BATTLES
FOR
US.

the world. On every page and in every story, Jesus can be seen—faithful, able, trustworthy, mighty, loving, worthy, and victorious.

JESUS IS DAVID IN THE STORY OF DAVID AND GOLIATH.

As long as our eyes are stuck on the problem—the giant—and as long as we think the answer is up to us, the fight will not end. But all that changes the day Jesus steps into our Valley of Elah. It ends the moment we stop staring at our giant and lock eyes with Jesus instead. It ends the moment we understand we aren't the answer—He is.

In the story of David and Goliath, God didn't want the victory to happen because David had the best armor, the sharpest sword, and a whole army at his back.

God wanted the victory to happen simply because one young man trusted in Him.

THE POWER OF WORSHIP

All through this book, and throughout our fight, worship is going to be the playlist that leads us to victory. Because, ultimately, this is a book about worship.

WHAT A DIFFERENCE A TWIST MAKES

When you think about the story of David and Goliath, have you ever imagined yourself as David? The one taking down the giant? Imagine instead that Jesus is the One marching out to battle *for you*. How does that change the way you think about your own giants and how tough they are?

_____

_____

_____

_____

_____

_____

_____

_____

Maybe you're thinking, *Wait a minute. I need a book about fighting giants, not a book about church songs and music.* But worship is more than songs. Worship is like a magnifying glass—it lets us see God better. And that's especially important when we're facing a giant.

Sometimes we think worship is just for the times when God does something good or when something works out for us. It's like it's our way of saying thank you to God. But God is worthy of our praise *all* the time.

JESUS IS ON YOUR SIDE. HE IS FIGHTING FOR YOU, AND HE HAS ALREADY WON.

My friend Nan was in a terrible accident recently. As a result, she lost her right leg and her father. It was heartbreaking. Yet, as soon as she was released from the hospital several weeks later, she was at church with her arms raised worshipping Jesus. Why? Because even though she was going through the worst days of her life, God was still her Savior, her hope and strength.

When we face giants, it's easy to let our eyes get glued to them. But when our eyes are locked on God, our giants' powers begin to flicker and fade.

When I was in the fiercest fight against my own giants—the giants of control and rejection—it was praising God that helped me fight. Before I closed my eyes at night, I would name the things I wanted to control, and then I would say to myself, *That belongs to God.* I would tell myself that if God wanted a certain thing to happen, it would happen. And if He didn't, why would I? Then I began praising the One who is *actually in control.*

And my giants stopped talking. Or at least I stopped listening.

I don't know what worry or fear is keeping you up at night or making you want to stay under the covers all day. But I do know Jesus is on your side. He is fighting for you, and He has already won. That's not just words on a page. Jesus has, in fact, already defeated every giant. And He is inviting you to come and see what He has done.

But it's still a fight. Because even though you *know* your giant has been defeated, it can still feel like that Goliath is shouting insults at you.

JESUS HAS ALREADY WON

What worries or fears are keeping you up at night? Write them out here, and ask Jesus to remind you that He has already defeated these giants.

_____

_____

W.O.R.S.H.I.P.

What exactly is worship? Colossians 3:17 gives a pretty good definition: "Everything you say and everything you do should all be done for Jesus your Lord. And in all you do, give thanks to God the Father through Jesus" (ICB). In other words, God wants your entire life to be worship. How can you do that? Use the letters of the word *worship* to remind you of the different ways you can worship God each day.

W = *Watch* for all the good things God has done, and thank Him for them (Psalm 66:5).

O = *Obey* His commands to love God and love each other (Matthew 22:37–39).

R = *Read* His Word every day (Psalm 119:105).

S = *Sing* praises to Him (Psalm 95:1).

H = *Help* others (Hebrews 13:16).

I = *Invite* someone to learn about Him (Acts 4:20).

P = *Pray*, or talk to God, all the time (1 Thessalonians 5:17).

CHAPTER 2

Dead but Still Deadly

When I was a kid, I used to go to summer camp with my church at Hilton Head Island in South Carolina. We stayed at the Presbyterian campground, just across the main road from the ocean in an area that could only be described as "jungle-ish."

When I say "jungle-ish," I mean it was wild land overgrown with swampy forests. This was the 1970s, long before Hilton Head became the modern vacation spot it is today. The campground had a dining hall, a kitchen, and a rustic chapel. There were five girls' cabins and five guys' cabins. A long sandy trail led from the main area to the cabins. It was fine during the day, but we wouldn't walk that trail at night without a flashlight.

In the middle of each cabin cluster was another building where the bathrooms and showers were.

And that's where the fun started.

At night, if you needed to go to the bathroom, you had to scamper down the path to the bathroom. You never knew what sort of wildlife you might meet on the way. Lizards ran the place. Spiders were everywhere.

And then there were snakes.

Lots of snakes.

Venomous snakes.

You'd pray you wouldn't come across one on the way to the bathroom at night, or worse, that one might be waiting for you in the stall!

At the start of each week, some kids would take one look at those bathrooms and decide *not* to make that journey at night, no matter the cost.

Despite the spiders and snakes, I loved camp. I can trace so many special steps of my early walk with Jesus back to that place. When I was in college, I became a counselor, so I got to spend a whole month on Hilton Head Island.

One of the counselors' jobs was to spread lime (ground-up limestone rock) around each of the cabin areas. Snakes supposedly hate lime. Sometimes the lime worked, and sometimes it didn't. When campers saw snakes on the bathroom trail, that meant we counselors needed to up our game. Some snakes are extremely dangerous, and we didn't want anyone to get bit. So on weekends when campers were gone, my best friend, Andy Stanley, and I took matters into our own hands. We'd grab a buddy or two and search for venomous snakes that lived near the cabins.

Our hunts went like this. Once it got dark (snakes like to move when the weather cools), we'd head out into the overgrown areas between the cabins, flashlight in hand. It didn't take long before a three-foot-long copperhead would cruise through the grass in front of us.

Once we spotted a snake, we'd glance around to make sure the copperhead's brother wasn't right behind him. Then we'd smack the snake on the head with a baseball bat. (Don't try this at home. This was really dangerous, and we should have just called animal control.) Once that snake was dead, we'd separate the snake's head—the dangerous part of the body—from its tail and bury it.

IT CAN'T HURT YOU.

We couldn't exactly leave the rest of the snake lying in the grass. So we'd swallow hard and pick the headless snake up by the tail. There's a strange thing about dead snakes, though: the head might be gone, but the body will keep squirming for a long time afterward. So we'd be walking around in the woods at night with dead snake bodies crawling up our arms. We all tried to be cool, but it gave me the creeps. I'd have to keep reminding myself that the snakes weren't actually alive. *Yep, I buried the snake's head. The snake is dead, Louie. The snake is definitely dead. It can't hurt you.*

But then another headless body would wrap itself around my arm.

Why am I creeping you out with tales of squirming headless snakes? There's an important reason, I promise. Because dead snakes are still dangerous. Just like dead giants.

THE DANGER OF DEAD GIANTS AND SNAKES

———

When a dead snake's body squirms, it might make the hair on your neck stand up, but that's all it can do: creep you out a little bit.

A dead snake's *head*, however, can still be extremely dangerous. Back on Hilton Head, we buried the heads of those dead snakes. Why? Because even after a snake dies and nothing is left but the skeleton, there is still venom in the fangs. If you're out walking barefoot and step on a dead snake's head, that spring-loaded fang can still shoot plenty of venom into your foot. That's big trouble.

Understanding the danger of dead snakes can help

us understand an important truth about Satan. He was defeated when Jesus died on the cross and rose again. The battle was over. The victory was won. That's all past tense. Thanks to His death, burial, and resurrection, Jesus has made Satan ultimately powerless. But for now, Satan can still wriggle and squirm and make the hairs on our necks stand up. Since we're not in heaven yet and the Enemy is still prowling around on earth, Satan can tell us lies that shoot poison into our minds and hearts. But we don't have to listen, because Satan is defeated and Jesus is our shield. However, if we *do* listen to Satan's lies, his poison will steal our hope and our joy. And it will make our lives so much less than what Jesus wants them to be.

RESURRECTION: to be raised from the dead, to be alive again

So there are two truths to keep in mind:

1. Satan was defeated on the cross. Jesus has won the victory. End of story.
2. Like the snake, Satan still wriggles. Satan still has venom.

Your giant is dead.

And yet . . .

Your giant is still deadly.

Maybe you're thinking, *Wait a minute. There's no*

way my giant is dead. In fact, he was beating me up just this morning. This giant is definitely still alive and punching.

I get that feeling. So let's figure this out together. When we struggle with our giants, we might pray something like, "Jesus, I've got a giant. Please do something about it right now! Please do something big!" We want something huge and supernatural and miraculous and brand new to happen.

YOUR GIANT IS DEAD. AND YET . . . YOUR GIANT IS STILL DEADLY.

But that's crazy because the fact is, Jesus already did something huge and supernatural and miraculous. He went to the cross. He died. He rose again. He defeated Satan and death.

Jesus died one time—*for all time.* Jesus never needs to die on another cross. Period. The work of defeating death and Satan's power is finished. Completed. Done. Our giants have fallen. Goliath is dead from a hit to the head.

In the very front of the Bible, in Genesis 3:15, God told us this work of Jesus on the cross would happen. When God cursed the snake (who was really Satan), God declared that Eve's offspring would one day crush the serpent's head. That offspring is Jesus. Jesus is the ultimate snake-crusher.

First John 3:8 says it this way: "The reason the Son of God appeared was to destroy the devil's work." Jesus is not some puny, helpless god. Jesus came to earth to crush the power of sin and death. And that's what He did. The work is finished.

Yet even though Satan was defeated on the cross, he can still harm us. He is still dangerous. First Peter 5:8 warns, "Stay alert! Watch out for your great enemy, the devil. He prowls around like a roaring lion, looking for someone to devour" (NLT).

I meet so many people who love Jesus. They believe in Him. They want to follow Him with everything they've got. Yet they're still putting up with some sort of giant in their lives. That giant is torturing them, and it's taunting God. The evil power that fueled the giant has long been crushed. But they didn't know to watch out for dead snake heads. They went walking in the woods at night, and the fangs shot venom into their feet.

AS FOLLOWERS OF CHRIST, WE AREN'T LEFT POWERLESS.

The good news is that as followers of Christ, we aren't left powerless. James 4:7 tells that if we resist the devil, he will run from us. Of course, it's not really *us* that the devil is running from. It's the One who fights for us: Jesus!

RESIST THE DEVIL

To "resist the devil" (James 4:7) is to say no to the temptation to do wrong things. For example, imagine that your soccer ball (which you aren't supposed to kick in the house) crashes into your mom's favorite picture. You might be tempted to lie and blame it on your brother. The devil would *love* that. Instead, resist that temptation and tell the truth. The devil can't stand the truth! What are some other ways you can resist the devil?

- There's a juicy bit of gossip going around, and you're tempted to listen and share it. Don't do it! Walk away!
- Everyone is laughing at the new kid. If you invite her to sit with you at lunch, the other kids might laugh at you too. Invite her anyway!
- You have no idea how to do the problems on the math pop quiz. It would be so easy to look at your neighbor's paper. Don't do it! It's better to get a bad grade than to cheat.

Resisting the devil isn't easy. But God doesn't ask you to do it all by yourself. He promises to help (1 Corinthians 10:13). Just ask Him!

JESUS IS MORE THAN ENOUGH

Our best defense against giants is to trust that Jesus is enough. *More* than enough. He is all we need. Jesus is not lacking or poor. He is rich in everything we'll ever need to follow God.

In the last chapter we talked about how one of the big twists in the story of David and Goliath is to think of David as Jesus. Jesus is the One who fights the battles for us. Yes, we do have to do our part too. We must follow Jesus' plan and obey God's Word. But it's always Jesus who brings the giant down. Not us.

One big problem we Christians often have is that we act as if everything depends on us. Sure, we believe in God and we believe Jesus saves. We believe that Jesus changes our lives. We believe it's all about grace and that grace is a gift from God. But . . .

- if we're troubled by fear or anger,
- if we're caught in the sticky spider's web of needing the approval of others,
- or if we're struggling to fight an addiction to video games or YouTube or the wrong kind of friends,

then we act like it's up to us to conquer the giant all by ourselves.

JESUS IS **ENOUGH**. HE IS ALL WE NEED.

We say, "God, thanks for saving me. But I'm good now." Or "Thanks anyway, God, but I can do this on my own."

If we truly want to change—if we truly want our giants to fall—then we have to trust Jesus. Completely.

Think of it this way: Imagine someone walked up to you one day and handed you a suitcase with a million dollars in it. You could do a lot of great things with that money. Not to mention buy a house with a huge pool and a waterslide. But what if you just let that suitcase sit in your room for the rest of your life? What if you never opened it? Would that gift do you any good? No! You have to use the money.

When we follow Jesus, He hands us unlimited riches, but we also need to use those riches. Here's what that looks like in Scripture:

> We have everything we need to live a life that pleases God. It was all given to us by God's own power, when we learned that he had invited us to share in his wonderful goodness. (2 Peter 1:3 CEV)

Read the first bit of that verse again. "We have everything we need to live a life that pleases God. It was all given to us by God's own power."

Stop right there. Focus on these three words.

"Everything we need."

That's our suitcase of money. Our unlimited riches. That's what we've been given in Christ. God has given us everything we need to live our best life for Him. All joy. All value. All purpose. All hope. All comfort. All power to resist temptation. All power to change. *Everything we need*.

Our job is to use the unlimited riches by depending on Jesus. Sure, that's not always easy to do. In our world we are taught to be proud, strong, and independent. None of those things is wrong, but when it comes to living for Jesus, we must learn to rest in Him, to trust and depend on Him.

TEMPTATION: an invitation to sin

Dan DeHaan, my teacher back in those Hilton Head days, said that trying to fully understand the riches of God was like following a trickling brook as it flowed downstream. Step by step, as you follow each babble and turn, you learn more and more about the little brook. Soon, the brook widens into a fast-moving creek and then into a mighty river. As you walk along the bank, you get to know the river better and better. Until one day you look up and the river has become an endless ocean.

That's how huge the riches of Christ are. In Philippians 4:13, Paul talks about how we "can do all things through Christ who strengthens [us]" (NKJV). Those are the riches of Christ at work. He is enough. More than enough.

Those riches include things like the strength to do what's right when everyone else is doing wrong. It's peace when you're worried and rest when you're tired. It's joy even when things aren't going your way. And it's Jesus' promise to never leave you, to stay right beside you every moment of every day.

And these riches are all yours when you decide to follow Jesus.

THINK ABOUT IT

What riches of Christ do you see in your life?

_____

_____

_____

_____

_____

_____

_____

_____

JESUS

IS

BIGGER

THAN

OUR

GIANT.

HOW A DEAD GIANT LOSES ITS POWER

So let's zoom in on this often-missed line in the story of David and Goliath. The verse is 1 Samuel 17:50: "David defeated Goliath with a sling and a rock. He killed him without even using a sword" (CEV).

Did you see that? David didn't even have a sword when he killed Goliath. The smack of that stone was enough. Goliath was already dead when he hit the ground. His mouth wasn't going to insult God anymore.

The very thing that had terrorized King Saul was silenced. Saul had nothing more to fear.

Here's what we need to learn from this: When it comes to you and your giant, don't *hide* your giant and *especially* don't hide the fact that it's dead. *Share* it. Tell a small group of trusted friends about your giant, and tell them how Jesus knocked it down.

WHENEVER WE HIDE A PROBLEM, WE GIVE IT MORE POWER OVER US.

Why? Because whenever we hide a problem, we give it more power over us. But when we confess it—when we share it with someone we trust—it loses that power. Confession shines the light of Christ

GOLIATH MUST FALL FOR YOUNG READERS

on the problem. And most of the time, when we confess something, people aren't all that shocked anyway. Usually they say something like, "Yeah, I kind of already knew you were struggling with that."

Here's another way we can bring the power of Jesus into our lives. Pick up the sword of the Spirit—the Bible—and read it out loud. Memorize its words so that the light of Jesus' truths constantly shine in our minds and hearts.

> JESUS AND HIS WORD WILL DO THE FIGHTING FOR US.

We don't need to argue with our giants. We don't need to "be a David" and pick up a slingshot. Because we're not battling our giant with our own strength and ability anymore. When we pick up the sword of the Spirit, we're battling the giant in the name of Christ. Jesus and His Word will do the fighting for us. That huge, ferocious giant might be coming at us with a sword, spear, and javelin, but Jesus is bigger than our giant.

And He's the God who knocks down giants.

USING THE SWORD

One of the best ways to use the sword of the Spirit—the Bible—is to memorize its words. That way, you always have it with you. You're always ready to defend yourself against any giants. Some great verses to start with are Proverbs 3:5–6, 2 Thessalonians 3:3, and 1 Corinthians 10:31—and, of course, John 3:16.

Pick a verse and memorize it. Here's a trick to help you. Write the verse on a card and read it out loud. Scratch out one word and read it again. Do you remember that one word? Keep scratching out one word at a time—reading it out loud each time—until you have it memorized! Once the verse is memorized, write it below!

_____

_____

_____

_____

_____

CHAPTER 3

Fear Must Fall

I travel *a lot*. So airplanes are like my second home.

But I know some people who don't fly often are afraid of being trapped inside a metal tube thirty-five thousand feet above the ground.

Take, for example, the nice woman in the seat behind me on a flight to New York City.

Let me just tell you that landing at New York's LaGuardia airport can be, uh . . . *interesting*. Parts of the runway stretch out over water, and it's *terrifying*. Then there's the weather. In winter (or even on a foggy day), landings at LaGuardia get really tricky. Recently a jet slid on the icy runway, plowed through a fence, and skidded to a stop with its body hanging over the open water. Glad I missed *that* flight.

Back to the story of the woman seated behind me. As we descended into New York City, I glanced out the window. But there was nothing to see except a thick, foggy blanket between us and the ground.

"Honey, I can't see the ground," the woman behind me said to her seatmate.

Now, I don't know if you've ever flown on a plane before, but you've probably ridden in a car when it was foggy outside. Fog can get so thick that you can't even see the taillights on the car in front of you. Imagine being way up in the sky and feeling that way! Scary, right?

A little later the woman spoke again. "How can we land if we can't see the ground?" Her voice quaked.

The plane lowered in the sky as we neared the airport. It felt like we were still a few minutes away from landing, but I didn't know for sure. What I *did* know was that the fog wouldn't last. A commercial airplane can't land if the pilot can't see the runway. And definitely not *this* runway that sticks out over the water. The fog would clear. We only needed to wait. But I don't think the woman behind me was an experienced flier. She didn't know the clouds were going to part. I could almost feel her hand holding tightly to the seat as her voice squeaked, "I still can't see anything! I can't see the ground!"

She was afraid, and I wanted to tell her it would all be okay. In just a few seconds, or minutes, the city would appear beneath us. But she didn't know me, and I don't think she would have listened.

In that instant the plane slipped through the final bit of fog. The rooftops of houses and businesses appeared.

She shrieked, "I see the ground! Oh, there it is. I can see it!" I could hear the relief in her voice. She felt safe again.

Here's the point of this story: fear grabs us whenever we believe something bad is going to happen and we can't do anything to stop it. Sometimes the fear is understandable, and sometimes it makes no sense at all. But no matter what kind of fear it is, it always affects us.

FEAR IS A BIG DEAL

Fear is a big deal in the story of us and God. The command to *fear not* is the most repeated commandment in the Bible. Someone counted 366 "fear nots" in the Bible—one "fear not" for every day of the year, including leap year. Plus, there are a lot of "cousins" to this commandment such as "Do not be afraid," "Take courage," and "Take heart."

Why is this commandment repeated so often? Because a lot of us have a lot of fears. Fear is one of the most common giants that must fall. Fear can taunt us, paralyze us, and control us. And while fear can never

DO

NOT

BE

AFRAID.

TAKE

COURAGE.

TAKE

HEART.

dim God's glory—nothing can do that—it *can* dim the way we shine God's glory into the world.

The tricky thing is that fear doesn't always look like fear. Yes, sometimes fear *is* flat-out terror. It's shake-in-your-boots fright. But at other times this giant sneaks up on you. It shows up as worry or anxiety or nervousness or stress or dread or stomachaches. Fear chews away at our confidence, robs us of sleep and rest, and steals our praise for God.

What do we do with these fears? How does this giant fall?

THE TRUTH ABOUT FEAR

First thing, let's remind ourselves of this powerful truth: the giant of fear can taunt us, but it doesn't have the ultimate power. Jesus has the ultimate power. Fear may pull our eyes away from God and crush our confidence. But the giant of fear is already dead. It's done for. It was conquered by Jesus on the cross. Now, in the name of Jesus, the giant of fear must fall.

That starts when we agree with God that the giant of fear is already dead. How? By focusing on Jesus. By studying His Word, seeing how He always keeps His promises. And by listening when He speaks through His Word. That's what builds up our faith, and faith is the cure for fear.

FAITH IS THE CURE FOR FEAR.

The opposite of fear is not being bold and courageous. The opposite of fear is faith. And faith begins when we say, "I believe God is bigger than this giant."

Faith isn't an instant fix, though. We might have been hanging out with the giant of fear for a long time, so it may take a while for it to leave. The answer is rarely as simple as saying, "I won't listen to fear anymore." Just like a fever can be a symptom of the flu, fear is a symptom of something bigger and deeper. To get rid of this giant, we need to dig deeper and figure out why we're afraid. And what I've learned is that it's usually for one of three reasons.

WHY ARE WE AFRAID?

1. We were trained to fear.

Some people grow up surrounded by fear and worry. Maybe you were born into a family of worriers. Your mom is a grand-champion worrier. Or your grandmother is. Maybe your father. Or your grandfather. You were barely walking when family members were like, "Oh my goodness, where's your coat? Bundle up tight, or you'll catch a cold."

"Don't get too hot."

"Don't swing too high."

"Don't forget your bicycle helmet."

"Don't talk to strangers."

It's one thing to be careful—being careful helps us stay safe. But sometimes, we act like life is one big threat that never goes away. At any minute, something could go wrong. If that describes you, then you need to *un*train yourself—or, rather, you need to train yourself *not* to fear. How? By trusting God. By reminding yourself that He is in control, and He is bigger and stronger than whatever it is you're afraid of. Like any training, this will take time and practice. But with God by your side, you can do it!

2. We're hiding something.

Any time we hide something we know we shouldn't, fear wins. Here's the pattern: We make a mistake. We do something wrong. But we don't confess it. Mostly because we feel embarrassed or ashamed. Or we don't want to be thought of as anything less than perfect. Or, let's be honest—we don't want to get in trouble.

IF WE CONFESS, FEAR WILL NO LONGER HAVE CONTROL OVER US.

So we hide our sin.

We choose to just live with the horrible feeling that someday whatever we've done will be discovered. We stuff our feelings of shame or embarrassment or perfectionism deep down inside us, and those stuffed feelings worm their way out of us in the form of anxiety. We think, *What if someone finds out about the real me? What if I mess up again? What will everybody think?*

Hiding mistakes, sins, and imperfections will drive us crazy. But if we confess those things when we pray and share them with someone trustworthy, like a parent or school counselor, then fear will no longer have control over us.

3. We want to be in control.

Some people want to control everything—their grades, sports, conversations, friends, and family. But soon they realize there's so much of life they can't control, especially how other people act. That's when fear, stress, worry, and anxiety come walking in.

When you are a controller, you really do go crazy, because you fear all the things you can't control. *What if something doesn't turn out the way I want? What if somebody messes up my plan? What if my friends don't do what I want them to do?*

Ask yourself this: What in your life have you ever really controlled?

THINK ABOUT IT

What things do you like to control? What happens when things don't go the way you planned?

_____

_____

_____

_____

_____

_____

GIANTS DON'T TAKE DAYS OFF

———

Spend some time talking to God—and listening. Be honest about what's in your heart. Can you see any of those three causes of fear in your life? Were you trained to fear? Are you hiding something? Do you fear the things you can't control? Or maybe it's all three!

Fortunately, you don't have to put up with the giant of fear. Take your fear to Jesus. Tell Him all about it. Then turn to the Bible and look at all the times God rescued His people when they were afraid. Like when He saved Daniel in the lions' den (Daniel 6). Or when God rescued Peter from that prison cell (Acts 12:5–17). Talking to God and trusting His goodness takes away the giant's power.

Let's take another look at the story of David and Goliath. There's something else I want you to see.

The Champion

First Samuel 17:4 says, "A champion named Goliath, who was from Gath, came out of the Philistine camp." Stop right there, because there's something important in that phrase. The word *champion* means that Goliath had a record. He had a history, and that's important because a lot of us have history with our giants. These giants didn't just show up this morning. They've been around for a while. Ever heard one of these taunts?

- *Remember when you came home from church and promised yourself that you were finally going to be brave enough to tell your friend about Jesus? Then guess what—you didn't.*
- *Remember that time you thought you were going to be all big and bold and stand up for that kid everybody makes fun of? But then the laughing and name-calling started, and you just walked away.*

- *Remember that time you decided you were going to turn away from those "friends" who always tempt you to do the wrong thing? Then, when it was time for lunch, you went right over and sat with them anyway.*

That's the voice of your Goliath. He likes to remind us of every mistake we ever make.

When Goliath faced the armies of Israel, he wasn't simply Goliath. He was Goliath, the champion from Gath. The Philistines let everyone know he was an undefeated warrior. *And* he came from Gath, a land of bullies.

For forty days, Goliath came out every morning and every night. He started the day taunting, and he ended the day taunting. Check out 1 Samuel 17:8–10: "Goliath stood and shouted to the ranks of Israel, 'Why do you come out and line up for battle? . . . Choose a man and have him come down to me. If he is able to fight and kill me, we will become your subjects; but if I overcome him and kill him, you will become our subjects and serve us.' Then the Philistine said, 'This day I defy the armies of Israel!'" In other words, "I defied you yesterday, and the day before and the day before and the day before, and I'm doing it again today."

Giants don't take days off.

Verse 11 shows exactly what giants do to us: "Saul and his men heard what Goliath said, but they were

so frightened of Goliath that they couldn't do a thing"
(CEV).

Fast-forward to verses 20–24:

> David left the sheep with another shepherd and set
> out early the next morning with the gifts, as Jesse
> had directed him. He arrived at the camp just as
> the Israelite army was leaving for the battlefield
> with shouts and battle cries. Soon the Israelite and
> Philistine forces stood facing each other, army
> against army. David left his things with the keeper
> of supplies and hurried out to the ranks to greet his
> brothers. As he was talking with them, Goliath, the
> Philistine champion from Gath, came out from the
> Philistine ranks. Then David heard him shout his
> usual taunt to the army of Israel. As soon as the
> Israelite army saw him, they began to run away in
> fright. (NLT)

Can you imagine what that must have been like?
Chances are, you don't have to imagine. You've been
there. We've *all* been there. We go to church and to
Sunday school. We sing the songs and listen to the les-
sons. And we decide to do all the right things. We decide
to "live for Jesus." But then Monday rolls around and
that same giant steps up, and we run away in fright.

It's like we're a ping-pong ball, bouncing back and

forth. On one side of the table, we fully believe in the power of Jesus to defeat our giant and change things for the better. But when we get knocked to the other side of the table, we give in to the giant. We can all hear the taunts:

- *You're too small. You can't do it.*
- *You've made too many mistakes.*
- *I'm undefeated. You don't have a chance.*
- *You're just like your mom . . . your dad . . . your sister . . . your brother.*
- *You can't change.*
- *Get used to it. Your life will always be this way.*
- *Face it: deep down, you don't even want to be different.*

What's the answer?

Well, it isn't "just try harder." The answer is faith. Our giants can taunt us, but they don't have ultimate power. Jesus has the ultimate power. When we put our faith in Him, Jesus does this amazing thing—He takes our little bit of faith and makes it grow. And your first step in putting the power of that faith to work in your life is saying, "I believe God is bigger than this giant."

I love Romans 10:17. It says, "Faith comes by hearing, and hearing by the word of God" (NKJV). That simply means that when we dive into God's Word, we will see that Jesus is enough and that God is bigger than giants. That builds up our faith. And just as David used a stone to knock down Goliath, our faith becomes the stone that shuts up our giant.

Our job is to *never* take our focus off of Jesus. The apostle Peter did—more than once, actually. Remember what happened during that storm at sea?

CAUGHT IN THE STORM

———

In Matthew 14:22–33, Jesus sent His disciples out onto the Sea of Galilee while He stayed behind. It had been a long day, and He just wanted to be alone with His Father. He said to His disciples, "You guys go ahead. I'll catch up with you later." They agreed, and Jesus went up on the mountain to pray. Evening came, and the disciples were out in the middle of the lake when a storm came up.

It was no small storm. The wind howled. Waves crashed. The boat was tossed about. The disciples were not sure they were going to live through it. That's when Jesus decided to walk out to His disciples on the water— right on top of the waves. When the disciples saw Him, they were afraid. They thought they were seeing a ghost! But Jesus called out to them, "Take courage! It is I. Don't be afraid" (v. 27).

JESUS
SAID,
"TAKE
COURAGE!
IT IS I.
DON'T
BE
AFRAID."

Peter, all big and bold, said, "Lord, if it's you . . . tell me to come to you on the water" (v. 28).

Jesus said, "Come" (v. 29).

Can you imagine that? The waves and wind and darkness were raging all around. But Peter looked toward the voice and stepped out onto the water. He started walking toward Jesus. Then verse 30 says this: "But when [Peter] saw the wind, he was afraid and, beginning to sink, cried out, 'Lord, save me!'"

Notice how Peter "saw" the wind. I have friends who sail, and they say you can see and hear and feel a gust of wind as it moves down the lake. A storm attacks all our senses—in the same way the giant of fear can attack us. We *feel* fear in the pit of our stomach. We *hear* fear in the terrible things we say to ourselves. We *see* fear as we either imagine the worst happening or watch it happen in front of our eyes. What Peter experienced—through all of his senses—paralyzed him with fear, and he began to sink. That's when he cried out for Jesus to save him. Verse 31 says, "Immediately Jesus reached out his hand and caught him. 'You of little faith,' he said, 'why did you doubt?'"

Why did Peter doubt? Those waves were huge! The wind was battering Peter. Sheets of water flew over him. And then there was the whole walking-on-water thing. Peter realized for a second he didn't normally do that. Thoughts of drowning probably flashed through his mind.

But there is good news. As soon as Peter said, "Lord, save me!" Jesus *immediately* grabbed him. There was no hesitation. No delay.

YOU HAVE NOTHING TO FEAR.

The storm didn't stop immediately, though. No, the storm was still raging when Jesus caught Peter. On the way to the boat, I think Jesus probably said to Peter, "It's okay. I've got you—even in the middle of this storm. You have nothing to fear." And Jesus says that same thing to us.

So what do we need to hear and see and feel and understand to know that Jesus has got us too? Four things. Four things that—with the power of Jesus—will make the giant of fear fall.

KNOCKING DOWN THE GIANT OF FEAR

1. Remember God is able.

God is able. Period.

God is able to get rid of our giants. Now, we may have been living with this giant of fear for months and even years, so it may take some time to knock it down. Or it could happen in an instant. Because God is able to do that.

God often works through others to take down our giants. Remember Lazarus? The guy Jesus called out of the grave (John 11)? He came alive in an instant. But when he walked out of that grave, the people around him needed to unwrap his grave clothes. To get rid of your giant, you may need some people to help you. Maybe it's a parent, teacher, pastor, counselor, or trusted friend.

But no matter how our giant falls, the first step always begins with believing and declaring this truth: "My God is able to save."

In Matthew 6:25–34, Jesus asked,

> Why do you worry about what you'll eat? Or what you'll wear? Will worrying add one inch of comfort to your life? Your Father will give you what you need because He is able. (author's paraphrase)

God uses His Word to remind us that He is able. As we study and memorize His words, they will replace in our brains what we are afraid of. A storm might be raging around us. A giant might be taunting us. But we can turn to the truths of God's Word and remind ourselves that God is able. He is always able.

2. Keep your eyes on the Lord.

I love Psalm 16. It was written by the shepherd boy, David. The whole psalm is great to memorize, but especially verse 8. David said, "I keep my eyes always on the LORD. With him at my right hand, I will not be shaken."

PSALM 16

Take a couple of minutes to read Psalm 16. Read it out loud. It's not long, only eleven verses. Now, make it your own by memorizing it. Today, start by memorizing verse 1. Tomorrow, add verse 2, and then each day add another verse. Notice which verse touches your heart most each day.

Isn't that great? Why did David not feel terrorized by the giant? Because David constantly focused on Someone bigger than Goliath. He kept his eyes, his thoughts, and his focus on the Lord. Because God was at David's right hand, David would not be shaken.

Yes, the giant was bigger than David. But God was bigger than the giant.

Now, check out that term *right hand*. In the Old Testament, it was a position of great honor. If you sat at the right hand of someone, then that was the best seat in the house. In the New Testament, those who believe in Jesus are even closer to God than His right hand. That's because His Spirit actually lives *in* those who follow Him

(Galatians 2:20). Jesus lives in us when giants taunt us. Jesus lives in us when we are in the middle of a storm. And because Jesus is there, we will not be shaken.

3. Name the fear that's keeping you up at night.

Anxiety can be crushing, but I've learned that anxiety is not the real problem.

GIVE GOD YOUR FEARS

What is making you anxious? What is keeping you up at night? Once you can name it, let's give it to God. How? Well, this might seem a bit strange at first, but trust me, it's helpful. Close your eyes. Imagine holding your fear—whatever it is—in your hands. Now lift up your hands to God and offer that fear to Him. Imagine Him taking it away. Trust Him to take care of it and to take care of you. Feel that peace? That's God telling you, "Don't worry. I've got this."

We are anxious for a reason. Something, or someone, is making us anxious. To be free from fear we have to name the specific things that are making us anxious. And we have to tell God about them. This doesn't have to be something complicated or fancy. Just tell Him.

Say, "God, this is what is making me afraid:

- "There's this big test coming up, and my parents expect me to get a good grade. But I don't understand the questions."
- "I finally earned a spot on the team. But now this new kid joined the team, and everyone says he's really good. Will I end up on the bench?"
- "My dad lost his job. Will we be okay?"
- "My mom's first chemo treatment is tomorrow, and I am so scared."

Once we name our fears, we can hand off those worries to God. We can place them in our heavenly Father's hands, and we can trust Him to take care of them. We're not saying there's no problem. We're just trusting that God is able to take care of it. We can leave our fears with Him and sleep in peace.

Like David, we say this:

> You, O LORD, are a shield around me;
>> you are my glory, the one who holds my head high.
> I cried out to the LORD,
>> and he answered me from his holy mountain.
> I lay down and slept,
>> yet I woke up in safety,
>> for the LORD was watching over me. (Psalm 3:3–5 NLT)

4. Fill your heart, mind, and mouth with praise.

When we keep our eyes on Jesus, we're always ready to sing His praises. Maybe you're thinking, *But why would I sing when I'm still in the middle of the trouble? When I'm still afraid of what might happen?*

We're either thinking about doom and destruction, which kicks our fear into high gear. Or we're reminding ourselves of the size, power, and love of God. We trust that His plans for us are good (Jeremiah 29:11).

The cure for fear is faith, and the playlist of faith is worship.

WHAT'S YOUR PLAYLIST?

Create your own worship playlist by starting a list of your favorite songs and verses.

_____

_____

_____

_____

_____

WHEN YOU'RE LOST IN A STORE

How can you know the giant of fear has fallen? It's when you can rest without worrying. What does that look and feel like?

Think back to when you were younger. You were with your mom in a store, and you were old enough that she didn't need to hold your hand every second. You had a little freedom to explore, so you went a few feet away, and that was all right. Then you went a few more feet away, and that was all right. You could still see Mom. Then you went a few more feet away. You were feeling pretty good about yourself then. Four years old and checking out the shoe section all by yourself. But then you turned to look for your mom, and suddenly you couldn't see her anywhere. Remember that feeling?

Uh . . . "Mom?"

You called a little louder, "Mom!"

Still nothing.

You looked up and down. You looked left and right. Your heart started to beat hard, and you were close to a meltdown. You rushed down one aisle and up another. "Mom? Mom!" *Where can she be?*

You dropped to the floor and searched for her shoes under the racks.

Then you just let loose and wailed. You were crying because you felt lost and scared. Because you lost sight of the one who cares for you.

And then you heard it.

Her voice.

"Over here, baby," she said.

She knew where you were. She was watching for you. Waiting for you. Wanting you to refocus and put your eyes back on her.

That's what it feels like to rest in safety. We are found again. We're right where we're supposed to be.

And this is what God is inviting us to do—to be constantly aware of His presence. To focus on Jesus. To remember that God is able. That He is always with us. And that He is always good.

GOD IS INVITING US TO BE CONSTANTLY AWARE OF HIS PRESENCE. TO FOCUS ON JESUS.

The battle against fear is not ours to fight. The battle belongs to the Lord. Jesus has already taken the sling and the stone and killed the giant. The giant of fear has already fallen. Our responsibility is to have faith. That's the cure for fear. God is able. Jesus is enough. When we keep our eyes on Him, we will not be shaken.

GOD IS ABLE

Writing helps us remember things in a way that just saying or thinking them doesn't. So take a few minutes to remind yourself of what God can do. Write your fears, and after each one, write what God is able to do with that fear.

I fear _____, but God is able to _____.

I fear _____, but God is able to _____.

I fear _____, but God is able to _____.

I fear _____, but God is able to _____.

I fear _____, but God is able to _____.

CHAPTER 4

Rejection Must Fall

Rejection is real.

Nobody wants to feel like he or she isn't good enough. Or smart enough. Or wanted enough.

Nobody wants to be left out or overlooked.

We may pretend we don't need anyone else's approval. But even if we wish it wasn't true, other people's opinions matter to us. A word of rejection—even a small or accidental one—can sting.

Maybe you actually were rejected. And that feeling is like a cold wind that follows you wherever you go.

- Your parents split, and you're having to figure out how to live with being shuttled between families.

- Your best friend decided you weren't friends anymore.
- Someone you loved suddenly died.

Your feeling of rejection could be big and easy to see. Or it could begin with something small, something that seemed harmless at the time.

TENNIS ACE

When I was a teenager, I dreamed of becoming a professional tennis player. My high school years were all about practicing. Every day we hit tennis balls. In the winter. In the rain. In the heat. At night. Against the side of a wall. We hit tennis balls *all the time*.

In my senior year I made the number-one-ranked doubles team for our school. I could hold my own in doubles, but the real reason we were number one is because my partner was Ray Dukes, the best player on our team.

Ray and I battled all spring long and made it all the way to the regional finals match. If we won, then we'd go to state. In the middle of that match, I looked up and saw my dad watching me. He'd never come to see me play before because our matches were always in the afternoon when he had to work. Now, my dad's nickname for me was Ace. (It had nothing to do with tennis. He just liked the name, and I did too.) And I was serving at the very moment I spotted my dad. I figured it must be a sign from God, because I was about to blow my opponent away with my best serve.

In tennis, you get two chances to serve each point. If you miss the first serve, it's called a fault. It's okay if you miss because you get a second serve. But on your second serve, you've got to make sure the ball is in, or it's your opponent's point. That's called a double fault.

I knew exactly what I was going to do. With my first serve, I was going to drive the ball so hard my opponent wouldn't even see it coming, much less touch it. My dad was going to see me make this awesome serve, and he was going to think, *Wow! Way to go, Ace!*

I bounced the ball three times, tossed it high over-head, and gave it everything. *Bam!*

Ten feet over the back line. Out.

A bead of sweat dripped off my forehead. I swallowed hard and didn't dare look at my father. Again, three bounces, toss, and . . . *smack!*

Straight into the bottom of the net. Double fault.

One point for the other team.

I tried to shake it off and be ready for the next serve. It didn't work.

Serve after serve. Miss after miss. Fault. Double fault. I bet I double-faulted ten times that day. It was brutal.

The only good news? Somehow we fought and clawed and ended up winning the match. We were going to the state tournament after all.

We were pumped.

Later that night, I was eager to share the victory with my dad. He'd left right after we won to get back to the office, and I hadn't had a chance to talk to him. I pictured him saying, "Hey, tough match. But you kept playing your guts out. Way to go. I'm proud of you, Ace."

It didn't turn out quite like I had planned.

Instead, my dad chuckled and said, "Well, I don't think we can call you Ace anymore. From now on we're going to call you Double Fault." He said it with a smile, and I think he meant it in the best way he could, but it stung. It really stung. The crazy part is that even today—years later—there are times when I go to serve the ball that I still hear my father's words in the back of my mind:

We're going to call you Double Fault.

I know someone is thinking, *Seriously, you're telling me that your dad's one comment was a big issue for you? Wow, what a wimp.*

I get it.

For some of you the rejection is way worse. It's like Mount Everest. Huge. Real. And devastating.

But this story is about more than a kid playing tennis. It's about how the giant of rejection can grow in a person's mind and heart. My dad didn't mean to reject me that night. Nope, he was an amazing dad. His words were innocent. After all, I had double-faulted—*a lot*!

But even when no harm is meant, a tiny seed of rejection can be planted and grow up into a giant.

TWO BRANCHES ON THE SAME FAMILY TREE

Rejection shows up in more ways than we might think. This giant has cousins on both sides of the family tree— and they don't look anything alike.

On one side of the family, the cousins are called *insecurity* and *low self-esteem*. It's that feeling that we're never quite *enough*, never as good as everyone else. For some of us, it might turn into hating ourselves.

On the other side of the family—this might surprise you—the cousins are *perfectionism* and *overachiever*. It's that drive to succeed and win, no matter what the cost.

Both cousins are part of the same unhealthy family. If you've been told you're worthless and nothing special,

WE'VE ALL HAD THAT FEELING THAT WE DON'T MEASURE UP.

then you feel bad about yourself. And if you've been told you're only valuable when you get all As or win the trophy, then you think you've got to prove yourself every single time to be accepted. Both are part of the giant of rejection.

All of us battle some sort of rejection. We've all had that feeling that we don't measure up. We all face times when we feel like we need to work hard to prove our worth. We see signs of this everywhere today, especially on social media.

ONLY IF

When I was a kid, there were maybe twenty other kids in my class at school. That's basically all the people I had to compare myself to. But today, thanks to social media, we've got an endless number of people to compare ourselves to. And let me tell you this: every time people post something, they're basically asking, "Am I good enough? Do you like me or not?"

I'm guessing some of your parents aren't letting you have your own social media accounts just yet. Honestly, that's a good thing. But it's never too early to get ready for the way things work in the world of Instagram and YouTube.

When do we get the "likes" on social media? It's often "only if."

- *Only if* our hair looks amazing.
- *Only if* we went to the right party or the right concert.
- *Only if* we're hanging out with the coolest crowd.
- *Only if* we made the winning shot.
- *Only if* we were the star.

Then and only then will we get the "likes." *Hello, world, this is me—do you like me?*

Only if.

Here's something really important we all need to remember: Pretty much no one posts selfies of the real world. "Hey, world, I just woke up. My hair is a wreck, and my face is covered with zits!" We don't post selfies when we come in third (or twenty-third) or when we're hanging out with ordinary friends in ordinary sweats. I mean, sure, we take selfies sometimes to talk about what a bad day we've had. Sometimes we make fun of our failures. But even then we're usually fishing for a compliment. We want someone to tell us we really are awesome.

Social media can be a good thing when used in the right way. But if social media is where we're finding our value, then we're sunk. If we live for people's approval, we will die by their rejection.

IF WE
LIVE
FOR
PEOPLE'S
APPROVAL,
WE
WILL
DIE BY
THEIR
REJECTION.

God made you just the way you are. He doesn't compare you to others. God put a special and unique gift within you. And we can't be so busy chasing or scrolling after everyone else's life that we miss out on the one God gave us.

Others might make fun of you or try to cut you down. That's not about you. It's about them. They are trying to make themselves feel more important by making you feel less important. But you're not going to let that giant of rejection win! Why? Because you know you are God's special person, His prized son or daughter.

If we're not careful, we will forget we were miraculously created by God. We were each made for a purpose, and He has a plan for our lives. God doesn't want us comparing ourselves to others or running someone else's race. He said, "Run *your* race" (1 Corinthians 9:24 TLB, emphasis added). Period. When we lose sight of the miracle of our creation, then we're going to be tortured by the giant of rejection.

DAVID GETS REJECTED

When David came to the battle against Goliath, he was up against the giant of rejection—not once but three times. It's right there in our text.

Rejection #1:

At this time David was still a teenager. He wasn't in the army; he was taking supplies to his brothers. When he got to the camp, he heard Goliath's taunting and didn't like what he heard. He asked who this giant was and who was going to take him down. But look at what the Bible says: "When Eliab, David's oldest brother, heard him speaking with the men, he burned with anger at him and asked, 'Why have you come down here?'" (1 Samuel 17:28).

Let's back up a step, because Eliab's anger isn't surprising if we know the rest of the story. In 1 Samuel 16, we see that David had seven older brothers. When the prophet Samuel came to Jesse's house to anoint a new king for Israel, Jesse (David's father) first brought out Eliab. He was the biggest, oldest, and strongest. Samuel thought, *Surely he will be the new king.* But God said to Samuel, "No, not him."

How about the next oldest brother?

Nope, not him either.

The next?

Nope.

And on down the line. David was so young that Jesse left him out tending sheep. But Samuel asked to see him. And when David arrived, God said to Samuel, "That's the one. Anoint him."

How do you think Eliab felt that day? Surely he was jealous. The oldest was always the chosen one. But he wasn't chosen as king. The youngest brother was. The kid who wasn't even in the lineup.

God chose the youngest of all as a way of showing that outward appearance doesn't matter to God. A heart of faith does.

In a perfect world Eliab would have been proud of David when he showed up at the battle. Eliab would have said, "Hey, everybody, this is my little brother. He's going to be the king of Israel one day. I get to be the older brother of the king—isn't that amazing?" Then Eliab would turn to David and say, "Man, I'm glad you're here, David. Thanks for coming. Thanks for the bread and cheese." Eliab could have offered to fight to protect his brother. At the least, he could have encouraged David when he said he wanted a shot at Goliath.

> IF YOU'VE BEEN REJECTED, BE CAREFUL NOT TO PASS ON THAT REJECTION TO THOSE AROUND YOU.

But that's not what happened. Eliab was bitter. He felt like he'd been rejected, so he burned with anger and said to David, "What are you doing here, anyway? Who's taking care of that little flock of sheep out in the desert? You spoiled brat! You came here just to watch the fighting, didn't you?" (1 Samuel 17:28 CEV).

Eliab felt rejected. And here's something important for you to remember: rejected people reject people. If you've been rejected, be careful not to pass on that rejection to those around you.

Rejection #2:

The second time David felt rejected was after he said he wanted to fight the giant. King Saul brought David in to talk to him. Saul said, "You don't have a chance against him. . . . You're only a boy, and he's been a soldier all his life" (v. 33 CEV). In other words, "Hey, David, you're not good enough, big enough, or strong enough. You can't do this."

We've all felt this kind of rejection. Maybe it sounded something like this:

- "You're never going to do that."
- "Don't get any crazy ideas."
- "Don't get your hopes up."
- "You're never going to amount to anything."
- "You're not smart enough."
- "You're not talented enough."
- "You're not beautiful enough."
- "You're not worthy enough."
- "You're not wanted enough."

David didn't let the rejection stop him, though. He went out to fight the giant—and was rejected yet again. By the giant.

Rejection #3:

Goliath stepped closer to David, looked him up and down, and "saw that he was little more than a boy, glowing with health and handsome" (v. 42). The one who had come to fight him wasn't even a man yet. And Goliath hated him. "Am I a dog, that you come at me with sticks?" (v. 43). Then he cursed David and said, "Come here . . . and I'll give your flesh to the birds and the wild animals" (v. 44).

Are you kidding me?

First, David gets rejected because his older brother feels rejected. Second, David gets rejected by Saul because he's too small. Third, David gets rejected by Goliath because he's too young to fight. David can't win. He gets it from all sides.

REJECTION HITS US ALL

Everybody deals with rejection. It just hits each of us in different ways.

Some of us have amazing talents, but we don't try out for the team, the talent show, or the play because, well, what if we don't make it? We take the easy path of not trying because we think that's better than risking rejection.

Then there are the people who are determined to win at everything. They try to prove to everyone they're good enough, beautiful enough, worthy enough, and wanted enough. They won't rest until they are the first in the class, the captain of the team, the star of the show, the best at everything. But they're never happy because their self-worth is all based on what they can accomplish. They don't know what they'll do if they don't make the team or get the A. It's the same giant of rejection.

The other side of the rejection coin is acceptance. And we all crave it. That's why some of you have friends you know aren't good for you, but you hang around with them anyway. They're not encouraging you to follow God. They don't have the same values you have, but they accept you. That's not true acceptance. That only comes from God.

When you seek God's acceptance instead of the acceptance of people, everything changes. Peer pressure doesn't have a hold on you anymore, because you want to please God more than the popular kids at school. The fear of not fitting in or being alone doesn't have a hold on you because you know God is with you and He is good. Comparison doesn't have a hold on you because you know God created you and no one can replace you.

The only thing that helps us knock down the giant of rejection is to wrap ourselves in the true acceptance of Christ. How do we do that? By remembering four important truths.

TRUE
ACCEPTANCE
ONLY
COMES
FROM
GOD.

THE REJECTION GIANT

Where does the giant of rejection show up in your life? Is it when you walk into the lunchroom and wonder where to sit? Is it stepping up to the plate and listening to the other kids groan because they know you'll probably get out? Or is it staying up half the night studying so you can prove you're "good enough" by getting an A on the test? Write your rejection fears here. Then at the bottom of the list, write, "God is bigger than these giants, and I am important to Him simply because I am His."

_____

_____

_____

_____

_____

_____

_____

FOUR WAYS TO REJECT REJECTION

---

1. Understand that you are God's miraculous creation.

Do you know you are the handiwork of God—a masterpiece of His own creation? David knew he was. Just look at what the Holy Spirit inspired him to write in Psalm 139: "For you created my inmost being; you knit me together in my mother's womb. I praise you because I am fearfully and wonderfully made; your works are wonderful, I know that full well" (vv. 13–14).

That's a mouthful of giant-slaying truth right there. We are each amazingly and wonderfully made. God doesn't make mistakes. God doesn't make rejects. He makes miraculous creations. And one of them is you.

In order for this giant to fall, you need to wrap yourself around the fact that you are not random; God made you on purpose for a purpose. Even if not everyone loves you, even if you don't make the winning shot, even if you fail,

YOU ARE A MASTERPIECE OF GOD'S OWN CREATION.

and even if you feel sad or broken today, God loves you. He created you uniquely and beautifully, and He has an amazing plan for your life.

HOW GOD SEES YOU

—

I want you to try something. It might sound strange at first, but stick with me. Look in the mirror. What do you see? Do you see all the things you wish you could change? Now, imagine how God sees you.

Unique.
Beautiful.
Wonderfully made.
Created for a purpose.

That's who you really are. Don't let some giant tell you anything different.

2. Believe that Jesus chose you.

Jesus chose us to be His. We need to believe that *and* stay amazed by that truth. Ephesians 1:4–6 tells us how we got into the family of God:

Even before he made the world, God loved us and chose us in Christ to be holy and without fault in his eyes. God decided in advance to adopt us into his own family by bringing us to himself through Jesus

Christ. This is what he wanted to do, and it gave him great pleasure. So we praise God for the glorious grace he has poured out on us who belong to his dear Son. (NLT)

From the very beginning of time, God knew you, loved you, and *chose* you to be His. Before people decided whether or not you are good enough for them, God had already decided that He wanted you as His son or daughter.

3. Remember the price God paid to rescue you.

God paid an enormous price for you.

Ephesians 1:7–8 tells us that "[God] is so rich in kindness and grace that he purchased our freedom with the blood of his Son and forgave our sins. He has showered his kindness on us" (NLT).

The gospel isn't just something to talk about on Sunday morning. It tells us the one thing we need to know most—that we are so very important to God. Faced with choosing between an eternity without us and allowing His Son to die for us, God chose to rescue us.

WE ARE SO VERY IMPORTANT TO GOD.

Our worth isn't wrapped up in what we have or what we can do—even though we should always try to do our best. Our worth is forever tied to the fact that God loves us so much that He sent His Son to die for us. And that Jesus loves us so much that He came.

You are worth Jesus to God.

4. Live like you're already accepted, not like you're still trying to be.

Our giant of rejection is not going to fall until we admit that we desperately need to be accepted. Because the fact is, we were made to be loved and accepted by our heavenly Father. The good news is we don't have to work to get God to accept us. He already does.

We just need to live like we've been accepted by God and stop chasing after the acceptance of others. Sure, we want to be loved and liked. But we must not change who we are or *whose* we are to get someone to like us.

Here's something to think about:

In Matthew 3, Jesus was being baptized in the Jordan River when something powerful took place. When Jesus came out of the water, "the sky opened, and he saw the Spirit of God coming down on him like a dove. Then a voice from heaven said, 'This is my Son, whom I love; with him I am well pleased'" (vv. 16–17).

Here's the point: Jesus hadn't started His ministry yet, but His Father said He *already* loved Him. Jesus hadn't given a message, healed anyone, walked on water, or died on the cross. Yet His Father was already pleased with Him. God poured out His acceptance on Jesus *before* He did a thing.

Now, imagine your heavenly Father saying to you—for all to hear—"This one is Mine." Imagine Him whispering in your ear, "I really, really love you. I am already pleased with you!"

Because He does and He is.

CHASE THE ONE WHO'S CHASING YOU

David probably wrote Psalm 8 when he was a young shepherd boy, way before he ever fought Goliath. Just imagine David out in the fields at night, tending his flock by starlight. He wrote, "When I consider your heavens, the work of your fingers, the moon and the stars, which you have set in place, what is mankind that you are mindful of them, human beings that you care for them?" (vv. 3–4).

David was looking up at the heavens, and he was blown away by the message he saw there. God made all this—the sun and the moon and the stars and the heavens—and yet . . .

- He loves and takes care of us.
- He knows our names.

- He has chosen us.
- He's made us His sons and daughters.
- He is chasing after us to rescue us.

Think about how awesome this is. We get excited when we get picked first in PE. Yet the God of the universe cares for us!

David ends Psalm 8 with these words: "LORD, our Lord, how majestic is your name in all the earth!" (v. 9). Do you know why he ended the psalm this way? It's because the worship of God shuts down the giants. Rejection and worship cannot exist in the same place. It's one or the other—and David chose worship.

THE GOD OF THE UNIVERSE CARES FOR US!

David didn't get puffed up about the fact that God knew his name. Instead he turned his thoughts to praising God. It's like he was saying, "I know I'm loved, God, but what's really amazing is how majestic *You* are!"

That's why our giants fall. Our giants go down so that we can be set free, yes, but the main reason they fall is so God gets glory.

HOW MAJESTIC!

Take a look up at the heavens—on a starry night, on a cloud-filled day, or in the bright sunshine. The God who made all that knows *your* name, loves *you*, and watches over *you* always. Write your own psalm of praise to Him.

_____

_____

_____

_____

_____

_____

_____

CHAPTER 5

Comfort
Must Fall

It's hard to think of comfort as a giant, isn't it? I mean, usually comfort is a good thing, right? How could it taunt or hurt us? We like having a cozy home, easy friendships, and enough money to do the things we want. We like everything to go the way we planned.

And none of those things are deadly giants by themselves.

The trouble comes when we make being comfortable the number one thing in our lives. Even over obeying God. Jesus came to earth with a specific mission, and He left us with one too: *share the truth about Him.*

That's why comfort might be the sneakiest giant of them all. It's so easy *not* to see it. It's the giant that causes us to miss the very *best* God has to offer because we have settled for something that is only *good*.

Here's how comfort shows up as a dangerous giant:

- We don't work hard at schoolwork and chores because we'd rather play video games or watch TV.
- We want to try something new, but we don't know if we'll be any good at it, so we do nothing at all.
- We know our friends shouldn't be making fun of someone in class, but we don't stand up for the other kid because we want to fit in.
- We're so happy to make the team, but all the games and practices end up stealing our time with God.
- We start to think, *It's my life. I can do what I want.*
- We choose the good thing, like hanging out with friends, but miss the God thing, like reaching out to a new friend who needs to hear about Jesus.
- We think the sin in our lives isn't that bad, so we don't try to get rid of it.

We're not bullies. We don't cheat on tests or steal candy from the store. We tell ourselves that the wrong things we do aren't *that* bad and we can get away with

COMFORT
CAUSES
US TO
MISS
THE
VERY
BEST
GOD
HAS
TO
OFFER.

not working very hard. But those kinds of thoughts are why comfort can be such a deadly giant. I know people struggle with some horrible things, but sometimes it's not the horrible things that hurt us most. Sometimes choosing to not do a hard thing does the most damage.

OUT OF THE NEST

—

Each year on the porch of our house, some birds build their nests. A few years ago, those birds built the biggest nest I'd ever seen. It was the size of a basketball! My wife and I loved watching these birds work, especially the mother birds. They would build the nest, sit on the eggs, and hatch the baby birds. They would fly to-and-fro, collecting worms and bugs for the baby birds to eat.

Then one year something messed up their routine. You know what it was?

London. Our new dog.

London is a big dog, and dogs regularly need to do things in the yard. In our case, it was the side yard right next to the birds' nest. Whenever London came outside, the birds would get all upset.

This was especially true when those baby birds

needed to jump out of the nest and learn to fly. I'm sure those mama birds were thinking, *Wait a minute. This is not what we'd planned. Get that dog out of here!*

Even then, with the dog down below, the mother birds finally said to their babies, "It's time. You can fly. You're ready. Off you go." And out of the nest they went. Sure enough, somewhere between the nest and the ground, those baby birds figured out how their wings worked. As they flew off into the sky, it was like they were saying, "Hey, this is awesome! We're so glad we didn't stay in the nest."

This is a picture of our life in Christ. A nest is a good thing for a while. It's safe and comfortable, and all our spiritual baby needs are taken care of. But if we're not careful, then the giant of comfort tempts us to stay in the nest forever. Maybe we see a big dog below on the ground. Or maybe we're not sure if we can fly or not. But Jesus says, "Hey, you weren't made to live in the nest forever. You were made to get out in this broken world and

> JESUS CAME INTO THE WORLD SO HE COULD SEND US OUT INTO THE WORLD.

share the good news about Me. Yes, it's risky, but you're ready to fly. Off you go." And somewhere between the nest and the ground, we figure out that our wings work.

We see how Jesus came into the world so He could send us out into the world. We see how we're filled with His Holy Spirit and how we can be the hands and feet of Jesus. And we say, "This is awesome! We're so glad we didn't stay in the nest."

THE TAUNTS END TODAY

In 1 Samuel 17, we see how comfort kept the Israelite soldiers in their camp. They shouted their battle cry every day. They got suited up and stood on the front lines. They had God on their side, and they believed He is the one true God. But for forty days they chose the comfort of camp over the risk of facing the giant. Goliath would come out and yell and taunt and threaten. And the Israelites would all say, "Nope, not today. Too dangerous. Too uncomfortable. Let's go have lunch. Let's stay in the tents where it's safe. Maybe we'll do battle tomorrow." They let the giant call the shots and rule their lives.

BY THE POWER OF GOD, YOU CAN DO THIS. THIS GIANT WILL FALL.

We can act the same way today. We have our churches and our safe Christian friends. There's an entire camp of us hanging out together in our comfort zone. But the giant is taunting us. We are failing to accept God's challenge to go out and tell the lost world about Him. We say all the right things, but we don't go out and face the giants.

In one day David did what the whole army of Israel hadn't been able to do for a month and a half. It makes me wonder what God wants to do right here, right now, in our lives. Maybe we've been waiting for everything to be *just right* before we move. Here's the thing I think makes us really uncomfortable: we can't see the whole path God is asking us to follow—we can see maybe just a step or two for now. And that path probably won't feel familiar and comfortable at first. Yet He says, *By the power of God, you can do this. This giant will fall.*

And the giant of comfort falls when we remember four truths.

THINK ABOUT IT

What is God asking you to do that's outside of your comfort zone? What is one thing you can do today to say yes to God's plan?

_____

_____

_____

101

KNOCKING DOWN THE
GIANT OF COMFORT

—

1. Our faith grows when we're uncomfortable.

That's not really what we want to hear, is it?

Read Hebrews 11, the "hall of fame" faith chapter in the Bible, and you'll see what I mean. The very first verse says, "Faith means being sure of the things we hope for. And faith means knowing that something is real even if we do not see it" (ICB). Trusting and believing in something you can't see—that's not usually a comfortable thing. But that's when your faith will grow and when you can best see the wonders of God at work. Just ask Noah, who built an ark when no one had ever seen a flood. Or Abraham, who left everything he knew to go to a land God had only told him about. Or Sarah, who held her baby in her far-too-old-to-be-a-mama arms.

Or Jesus. He suffered far worse than discomfort so we could become the sons and daughters of God. If we're not careful, we may sing songs about the uncomfortable moment of Jesus on the cross while we live very comfortable lives. Can you name anything in the life of faith that's completely comfortable? Saying no to sin? Nope, not comfortable. Changing to be more like Christ? No, not comfortable. Reaching out to tell people about Jesus? No, not always comfortable either.

Faith grows when we're uncomfortable.

2. *It's all about the fame of God.*

The whole point of our lives is to spread the fame of Jesus.

The army of Israel wanted to stay comfortable. They had food, tents, and a really cool war cry. They had armor. They had little brothers to bring them more bread and cheese.

So they weren't moving.

Then David showed up and said, "Hey, Goliath, you're insulting my God and taking glory away from His name. That's got to stop right now."

In the New Testament, Paul said, "You must have the same attitude that Christ Jesus had" (Philippians 2:5 NLT). What was that attitude? Think about this: Jesus was—and is—God, with the full rights and power of God. Yet He stepped out of heaven and came to earth. He humbled Himself and became a man—a servant. Jesus obeyed God the Father and went to the cross.

Why did Jesus do this? *For the glory of God.* Of course God loves us and cares about us. But everything Jesus did was to point people to God. And that's what we are to do too. That's what it means to live for His glory.

3. We need to line up with God.

You're in school. You know what it means to "line up." You stand behind the leader and follow where he or she goes. Lining up isn't just for school, though. It's also for life. The question is, who will you line up behind? Who will you follow?

It's easy to line up behind the people around us. But God wants us to follow Jesus' example. God doesn't tell us to avoid the world because it's a risky place full of sin. Rather, He tells us to grab the sword of the Spirit—the Bible—line up behind Jesus, and get moving.

Who are you lining up with? Who are you following? Who helps you decide where you go, what you watch, what you do? Make sure it's Jesus.

4. Life is short.

Chances are, this isn't something you think a lot about. But the fact is, our lives are like the blink of an eye when you compare them to how long eternity is. So it's important for us not to waste any opportunity to give fame to God.

When David's three older brothers and all the rest of the army of Israel got to the end of their lives, I believe they all shared a big regret. They'd wasted forty days sitting on that hillside. They had the power of God with them. They could have moved forward if they'd wanted to. But they didn't. They chose comfort instead.

LINE UP!

Lining up with Jesus isn't something you can do one time and be done. It's something you'll need to do each and every day, several times a day. What can you do to line up with Jesus . . .

in the morning?

_____

at lunch?

_____

in class?

_____

with your friends?

_____

in the evening?

_____

What's the danger for us? It's that we do the same thing. We waste our days thinking, *I've got time. I'll read my Bible after I beat this video game. I'll stick up for that kid everybody makes fun of tomorrow—or maybe the day after. I'll invite my neighbor to church next week. I'll obey God when I'm older.*

The Enemy wants to keep us comfortable, then he can tempt us to waste our days. But we are not created to be a people of comfort. We are a people of faith. And God is saying, *The battle is already won. I want you to step out with Me right now, today. Don't waste a moment of your life.*

We live on a planet with billions and billions of people who've never heard of Jesus. That's why time is short. They've got questions, and we have the answer. We have Jesus.

That's what matters—letting Jesus be known. We don't have time to settle for being comfortable.

GOD IS BIG

Maybe you already feel a bit like that Israelite army. Maybe you feel like you've spent too much of your young life in your tent being taunted by your giant. Then listen to this good news: *God is big*, and He is able to bring

LIFE IS **SHORT**. DON'T WASTE A MOMENT.

GOD IS ABLE TO BRING GOOD OUT OF EVERY SITUATION.

good out of every situation. He is able to breathe new life into every heart. He is able to do "far more than we dare ask or imagine" (Ephesians 3:21 CEV).

God is big.

Say that to yourself a few times. Let the words roll through your mind and heart. *God is big. God is big. God is big.* Do you hear that voice?

It's the voice of the giant slayer.

It's the voice of the one who fights evil wherever it pops up.

It's the voice of the one who gives what she has to those who don't have.

It's the voice of the artist, the actor, or the sports star who shines God's light into the world, even if it hurts his or her career.

It's the voice of the babysitter, the lawn mower, or the dog walker who shows the love of Jesus when he or she works.

It's the voice of the student who sees doing his best on his homework as an act of worship.

It's the voice of the kid who honors God by honoring his or her parents.

It's the voice of the one who pushes out of his or her comfort zone and says, "I'm going to tell others about

Jesus no matter what the cost." This is what it means to follow Jesus. And we can do this because . . .

God is big.

The giant of comfort wants us to believe that life is all about us and what makes us feel good. But that is a lie. Faith is never just about us and our lives. And it definitely isn't about always being comfortable. In fact, God often asks His people to be uncomfortable. Not because He wants us to be unhappy, but because He wants us to experience the joy and power of "jumping out of the nest" and learning to be all that He created us to be.

> GOD HAS A PLAN FOR YOU AND YOUR LIFE—AN AMAZING AND WONDERFUL PLAN, FULL OF ADVENTURE AND PURPOSE.

God has a plan for you and your life—an amazing and wonderful plan, full of adventure and purpose. And He is inviting you to live out that plan. It won't always be easy or comfortable. Yet if you step forward in faith and trust God, He will always be there to help you on your journey.

I think that's the way David was thinking when he walked into the valley to meet Goliath. And that's what we can remember too—that God is big and His plan is bigger and more rewarding than comfort ever will be.

THE GIANT OF COMFORT

Are there giants in your life that you've gotten comfortable with? Are you taking the easy path instead of the one God wants you to take? Write out a prayer asking God to make your giants fall and to show you the next step in His plans for you.

_____

_____

_____

_____

_____

_____

_____

_____

CHAPTER 6

Anger Must Fall

Most people don't think of themselves as being an angry person.

"I don't yell at my dog or the kids I go to school with," they'll say. "I don't lash out at my brother or sister, and I don't throw things around the house."

But that doesn't mean anger isn't there. Sometimes it lurks underneath the surface, waiting for the right spark to set it off.

ANGRY DAYS

For me, it doesn't take long to figure out an area of my life where anger is a problem. It's bike riding. How could riding a bike make me angry? It's because I have to share the road with cars. (This is a grown-up way to travel, so don't take off into the road on your bike!) The problem is that bike riders and car drivers aren't known for getting along. Drivers don't like the idea that some dude is in their lane, slowing them down. It's an environment where anger can flare on both sides.

Just the other day I was riding along, minding my own business, when a car turned right in front of me. If I hadn't slammed on my brakes, I'd have plowed straight into him. I wasn't happy about that. In fact, I was pretty angry. I shook my fist at the driver and yelled at him to turn around and come back. But really, what was I going to do if he did? Fight him? Fortunately, he didn't come back.

Shaking my fist was just the symptom of my anger— the part that could be seen. But I needed to ask myself, *What is really making me so angry?*

What makes you angry? Is it getting bumped around in the halls at school? Or maybe you feel like the chores aren't fairly divided at home. Or maybe someone else gets the credit for your work—or blames you for his or her mistakes.

Now, I want to be really clear about this: anger isn't necessarily wrong. But if anger is uncontrolled, stuffed down, or directed at the wrong person for the wrong reason, then anger can do us a lot of harm. Scripture is clear that anger is a giant that can shut down God's plan for our lives.

Like I said, anger isn't always wrong, and Jesus Himself felt anger. He acted on this powerful emotion yet never sinned. He sometimes had strong words for His disciples. He threw the money changers out of the temple. He once walked into a dinner party and immediately began insulting the host—but for a good reason (check out the story in Luke 11:37–53). So Scripture shows that there's a time to be angry and a time to rightly show our anger. But that's not what we're talking about in this chapter. We're talking about when anger becomes a giant. Here are three ways this giant can pop up in your life:

ANGER IS A GIANT THAT CAN SHUT DOWN GOD'S PLAN FOR OUR LIVES.

- **Wrongly felt anger.** You feel angry about something that never even happened. Perhaps some friends made a joking comment. They were just kidding, but you took it too seriously. Or you believed they meant to hurt you, but hurting you was the last thing they wanted to do. You're angry—and you might do something because of your anger—but you don't have a real reason to be angry.

- **Rightly felt anger that's wrongly expressed.** You really do have something to be angry about, but the way you're expressing your anger comes out all wrong. Maybe what your friends did was wrong, but that doesn't make it okay for you to call them names.
- **Rightly felt anger that's never expressed.** You're angry—and you have a good reason to be—but you pretend everything's okay. You stuff your anger down inside yourself. You don't talk about it. But not dealing with your anger hurts your heart, it hurts the people around you, and it can even hurt your health.

There are a million reasons why people are angry today. People can be angry at their parents. At brothers and sisters and cousins. At second-grade teachers who tell them they won't amount to anything. At friends who betray them. At classmates who don't invite them to their parties. Anger can happen anytime we feel betrayed, overlooked, or slighted. We wanted something, or we hoped for something, and we didn't get what we wanted. Now we're angry.

It's amazing how harmful anger can be when it comes on the scene. The good news is that God has killed the giant of anger in our lives. It's dead. It may still be talking to you and me. It may still be taunting us. It may still have deadly venom in its fangs. But the giant of anger is already dead.

ARE YOU ANGRY?

How about you? What makes you angry? Take a look at the following list, and circle the ones that are true for you. I've used "dad or mom" a lot in this list, but you can put someone else in the story. A friend. A grandparent. A brother or sister. A coach. A teacher. A pastor. Or even God.

You might feel betrayed or put down or cheated. Maybe you wanted something but didn't get it. The first step to feeling better is to be honest about how you're feeling.

I'm angry because someone left me.

I'm angry because someone didn't want to be my friend.

I'm angry because someone picked somebody or something else over me.

I'm angry because someone hurt me.

I'm angry because my dad or mom left my family.

I'm angry because my dad or mom is too busy for me.

I'm angry with my dad or mom because he or she didn't take care of us.

I'm angry because my dad or mom is gone all
the time.

I'm angry at the family who stole my dad or mom
from us.

I'm angry with God because someone I love died.

I'm angry with my family for giving all the
attention to my problem sibling.

I'm angry because I was never good enough for
my dad or mom.

I'm angry because _____

_____.

ONLY GOD KNOWS

In the story of David and Goliath, I don't think David
was all that angry. Sure, maybe he was angry because
God was being insulted and nobody was doing anything about it. That's the right kind of anger. What I see,
though, is David being surrounded by some people who
were angry for the wrong reasons. Like David's older
brother Eliab. In 1 Samuel 17, when Eliab heard about
David's plan to face Goliath, the Bible says he "burned
with anger at him" (v. 28).

Think about it: Eliab already knew David was a special kid. The prophet Samuel had said David would be king. And David had killed a lion and a bear. He was a fantastic musician and songwriter. He did just fine taking care of their father's sheep. And in light of all that, when David came up to the battle, Eliab should have encouraged him. But instead, Eliab's heart *burned* with anger. His anger was wrongly felt *and* wrongly expressed. Eliab might have felt hurt because David was anointed as king, but he didn't have a good reason to be mad at David. Here's how Eliab expressed his anger—with words.

Eliab looked at David and asked him, "Why have you come down here? And with whom did you leave those few sheep in the wilderness? I know how conceited you are and how wicked your heart is; you came down only to watch the battle" (1 Samuel 17:28).

Can you hear the anger in Eliab's words? Look between the lines. Eliab was saying, "I am a fighting man. I am the head of the brothers. You tend sheep (and just a few sheep, by the way). Did you have to hire a little sheepherder to take care of your little sheep while you came up here where the big boys are today?"

This is what angry people do. They find a way to knock down the people around them. At the end of the verse, Eliab called David *conceited* (which means "thinking of yourself as more important than others") and said his heart was wicked. It's never a good idea to assume what a person is thinking or feeling. Only God knows what's in another person's heart.

ONLY GOD KNOWS WHAT'S IN ANOTHER PERSON'S HEART.

David didn't let the anger of Eliab slow him down, though. And that's a good example for us to follow. David marched out in the power of God's name and did what God called him to do. Eliab could have done that too. He wasn't going to be king, but he could have been a lot more than he was. Eliab could have been David's champion from the start.

Don't give up on Eliab, though. His happy ending is told in 1 Chronicles 12:9. Years after Goliath was killed, Eliab was given the position of third-in-charge of King David's army. Eliab was musical, just like his younger brother, and Eliab went on to become a musician in David's army (1 Chronicles 15:20). And finally, 1 Chronicles 27:18 says that Eliab, a brother of David (although he's called "Elihu" here), was eventually made the leader over the whole tribe of Judah. So I like to think that Eliab and David eventually became close friends. The Lord worked in Eliab's heart. He changed his ways, and he was rewarded.

FIVE KEYS TO CRUSHING ANGER

Maybe you're looking for an instant fix to your anger. You want to be changed overnight. God can do that—but He doesn't usually. God changes our lives little by little, bit by bit.

Goliath taunted the Israelites every morning and night. And the Devil is even worse. The Bible tells us that he is *constantly* on the prowl, looking for ways to devour us every day. Our best—our only—defense is to *constantly* fill ourselves up with faith.

We need to keep reminding ourselves that Jesus has already won. Then we need to talk to ourselves like God talks to us—with love and grace. We need to tell ourselves biblical truths. We need to align ourselves with God and follow His plans. Then, little by little, things change. We replace anger with reading God's Word and praying for the people we're angry at. We begin to see others the way Jesus sees them. We invite Christ to take control of our hearts.

Yes, Jesus has already done the real work on the cross, and the giant of anger has already fallen. The battle is over, but the struggle continues. And with God on our side, He will win

GOD CHANGES OUR LIVES LITTLE BY LITTLE, BIT BY BIT.

the victory for us, day by day by day. Our part in this struggle is to remember these five keys to crushing anger.

1. Remember that we aren't perfect.

When we are angry at someone else, we must understand that we aren't perfect either—and that God has already been angry at us. We don't like to think of God as angry at us. That's because when we think of God's anger—or "wrath"—we think of it like human anger. We picture someone strutting around a room, shaking his fist, and throwing things against the wall. But God's anger isn't like our human anger.

This can be tricky to understand, but God is both loving and full of wrath at the same time. He is loving because God is love (1 John 4:8). But God is also holy, which means He can't have anything to do with sin. The "little" sins we accept, He doesn't accept. This world is full of sin, which is why God is full of wrath. But because God loves us so much, He gives us a way to escape His wrath—Jesus. We are forgiven! So we should forgive others.

Psalm 85 says it this way:

> You have forgiven the sin
> and taken away the guilt
> of your people.
> Your fierce anger is no longer
> aimed at us. (vv. 2–3 CEV)

WITH
GOD
ON
OUR
SIDE,
HE WILL
WIN
THE
VICTORY
FOR US.

That's what we need to keep in mind. God has already forgiven so much in our lives. That helps us stay humble. That keeps us from thinking we're better than anyone else. That helps us forgive others.

2. Remember that God has made peace with us.

The second key to crushing anger is a lot like the first. God has always loved us, but He hated our sin, and He hated our wrong choices. He burned with anger over the way we treated Him. Yet God has made peace with us.

Isaiah the prophet called Jesus the "Prince of Peace" (Isaiah 9:6). This is good news for an angry world. Jesus is coming to us and saying, "I have authority from heaven to make peace with you. I could sit here and talk about your sins, but I'm not going to do that. I'm here to offer you a deal, to offer you peace, to offer you what no one else can offer you: salvation." How did Jesus make a way for us to be saved? Through His blood poured out on the cross.

Whenever we're angry, we need to remember the cross. All the anger and wrath of God landed on Jesus at the cross. That's why we sing about the cross at church. That's why we celebrate the cross. Because that's where God made peace with us.

3. Believe that God is our avenger.

You've seen avengers in movies. They're the heroes who try to right the wrongs of the world. But did you know that

God is the ultimate avenger? When we are wronged, a lot of us want to take matters into our own hands. We want to get our own revenge. We think getting even is going to make things better—or at least make us feel better—but it's like throwing gasoline on a fire. It only blows things up.

The right way to deal with anger is to trust God and His justice. He is the ultimate avenger, and He will make everything right—in His own perfect time and perfect way. It might happen today on earth or in the future in heaven, but justice will come. And God will be fairer about it than you and I could ever be.

> THE RIGHT WAY TO DEAL WITH ANGER IS TO TRUST GOD AND HIS JUSTICE.

Choosing not to get even with someone doesn't mean we just ignore our anger. We may need to talk some things out. There may be some consequences. We may have to walk away from a person or situation. But we trust God to defend us and right all wrongs.

Paul said it this way in Romans 12:14: "Ask God to bless everyone who mistreats you" (CEV). And in verse 17, he said, "Never pay back evil with more evil" (NLT).

So if someone hits us, what should we do instead of hitting that person back? You say you're hurt. That's fine. You step away; that's fine too. But then you let Jesus heal that hurt.

Jesus is bigger than our wounds and bigger than our sorrows. He is able to heal you.

Paul said in Romans 12:18, "Do your best to live at peace with everyone" (CEV). This is the same guy who had rocks thrown at him, was thrown in prison several times, was beaten with rods three times, and was whipped within an inch of his life five times. Yet he didn't call for revenge.

Paul called for peace. Jesus calls for peace. And you should too.

4. Forgive.

How does the giant of anger fall? When, with Christ's power, we forgive the person we're angry with.

Paul said in Ephesians 4:26, "Do not let the sun go down while you are still angry." In other words, don't go to bed tonight without dealing with any anger still in your heart. Forgive the person who wronged you.

That doesn't mean you're saying what the person did was okay. In fact, if someone did something wrong toward you, it's *definitely* not okay. Forgiving someone also doesn't mean everything goes back to the way it was before or that you'll be best friends forever. Maybe you will still be friends, or maybe you need to stay away from that person. That's okay too. Forgiving someone gives you a chance to heal. Because your hurt won't go away until you forgive.

JESUS IS BIGGER THAN OUR WOUNDS AND BIGGER THAN OUR SORROWS.

But forgiving isn't easy. Maybe the person you're angry with doesn't live close to you or you're not talking to each other anymore. Or the hurt seems too big to forgive. I get that. There are some horrible things done in this world. But you've got to let it go. And God will help you. Go to the Lord in prayer and say, "God, by the grace of Jesus, I want You to help me forgive this person. You forgave me. I want to forgive them."

Sometimes forgiveness takes time. We may need to forgive people more than once—even for the same hurt. Or they may refuse to accept your forgiveness. They may say, "I don't care." Or "I never did anything wrong." Or "It was your fault anyway." That's okay. If they don't want to hear it, talk to God about forgiving them. When you do, the giant stops taunting.

When we forgive, the giant falls.

5. Remember we are sons and daughters of God.

A lot of anger comes from feeling betrayed and unimportant. The person who hurt us might have been a classmate, a teacher, an older relative, or even a parent. Yet it's God's voice we should listen to and believe. And He declares that we are His sons and daughters. He has adopted us. He has *chosen* us as His own. In God's eyes, we are loved and adored.

The giant of anger goes down when we remember we are loved sons and daughters of God.

THINK ABOUT IT

Have you heard this old saying: "Remember who you are and whose you are"? Well, who are you in Christ? Whose are you? And what kind of person does that make you want to be?

_____

_____

_____

_____

_____

_____

_____

FINALLY *FREE!*

___

One thing is for sure: we live in a broken world where lots of bad things happen, and that gives us plenty of reasons to be angry. But being angry and allowing this giant of anger to steal our joy are two different things. We have to get fed up with the giant and take it down.

Aren't you tired of being mad all the time? Tired of holding a grudge? Tired of constantly feeling tense?

Taking down this giant is really about letting go of control.

You see, anger tricks us into feeling we are in control. We think, *I'm not going to forgive. I'm not going to let you get away with it. I'm not going to ever speak to you again. I'm going to make you regret ever doing that to me.* And that makes us feel in charge. Yet half the time the other person doesn't even know we're angry—or doesn't care.

TAKING DOWN ANGER IS REALLY ABOUT LETTING GO OF CONTROL.

The saying "Let go and let God" has always bothered me a little. It seems too simple. But it's really true and quite powerful. And it's the best way to knock down the giant of anger. We have to let go of our anger and let God take care of making things right. What God did *for us*—sending Jesus to suffer so we could be saved from God's anger—is greater than what anyone could ever do against us. To be loved, to let go of the wrong things someone has done to us, and to let God put out the fire of anger sets us free. Free to live our lives, to run our race, to grow into who God says we can be.

WRITE IT OUT TO FIGURE IT OUT

Anger needs to come out—whether it's rightly felt anger or not. But it's super important to make sure it comes out in ways that are helpful, not harmful. Writing out your thoughts is a great way to express your anger *and* help you figure out what God wants you to do with that anger. It can be in a journal or in the space below. As you write, ask God to help you see if your anger is rightly felt. If it is, ask God to help you express your anger in ways that make the situation better, not worse. And ask God to help you forgive the person who wronged you. If your anger isn't rightly felt, ask God to change your heart and help you let that anger go.

_____

_____

_____

_____

_____

CHAPTER 7

Addiction Must Fall

The scene at the restaurant the other night was classic . . . and typical. Sitting at the table next to us was a mom, a dad, and three kids. I'm not sure how they ordered and ate their food because they were all in their own worlds. Dad was on his phone, answering emails. Mom was on Facebook, clicking and commenting on other people's lives. One of the kids was playing some game on his tablet. Another kid was turning his iPad from side to side, playing a racing game. The third kid actually had on headphones and was playing some sort of war game, destroying cities.

Addiction to electronics is a real thing. I recently read about a kid who was so addicted to gaming, he refused to eat or sleep for days because he couldn't stop playing. Eventually, he had to be admitted to the hospital!

News flash: we are an addicted generation. We don't think of ourselves as addicted, but we are. Maybe that's because as soon as we say the word *addicted,* we start thinking about the "big" addictions, like alcohol and drugs. But the truth is, we're addicted to all kinds of things. Some little stuff, some big stuff.

The big addictions are real. I'm not taking them lightly. Yet I don't want any of us to sit back and say, "Well, since I'm not struggling with this big addiction or that big addiction, I really don't have any addictions in my life."

We need to rethink what an addiction really is.

An addiction is anything we can't live without.

It's a habit we can't break.

It's a person we can't stop hanging out with.

A pattern we can't change.

That's the giant of addiction. It robs us of our very best life. And it dims the fame and glory of God in our lives.

That's why the giant of addiction must fall.

THE BIGGEST ADDICTION OF ALL
———

Addictions are powerful, and they usually don't make a lot of sense. I mean, why would we choose to do things that hurt us? But that's exactly what we do.

The thing we're addicted to is different for different people. For some people, it's video games. For others, it's the internet or YouTube.

Success can be an addiction too. You bring home all As and your GPA is 4.0. But that's not enough. You always need to come in first, and you can't handle it if you don't.

Even being "on the go" can be an addiction. You can't sit around and do nothing. You always want something planned, like practices every night and hanging out with friends every weekend. You'll do anything to avoid having nothing to do.

Some people are addicted to other people. You need a certain person, and if you don't see or hear from this person, then you get stressed. You know who you are. You're reading this book right now and wondering why your best friend hasn't called you. *Doesn't she like me anymore? Doesn't he want to hang out with me anymore? Why was she talking to someone else at lunch?* But . . .

Do you know what the most widespread addiction of all is? It's this: the approval of others.

If you just whispered, "Well, I'm not addicted to approval," then you actually are. People who say, "I don't care what you think" are actually saying, "It matters a lot to me what you think." Otherwise, they wouldn't feel the need to say they don't care! Hey—we all want to be liked by other people. We all want to be accepted. We all want to know we're not alone in this world.

Social media has figured this out. Today it's Instagram and YouTube. Tomorrow it may be something else. But the addiction of approval isn't going anywhere.

WE ARE ALL VULNERABLE

Underneath any addiction—or need for approval—is a bigger question: What hole in our lives are we trying fill up with this addiction? See, the games, the internet videos, the food, and the friends are only a symptom. The real cause of the addiction is something else—usually pain. Somebody rejected us. Somebody hurt our feelings. They made us feel like we're not good enough.

VULNERABLE:
easily wounded or hurt, easy to attack

We are lonely, angry, tired, frustrated, afraid, betrayed, lost, disgusted, sad, or just plain upset. *That's* the cause. The addiction is whatever shows up and promises to make us feel better.

And maybe that addiction actually does seem to help for a little while. But then the addiction lets us down big time, and we feel worse than ever. Think of it this way: When some kids feel sad or lonely or angry, they look to food to make them feel better. If you've had a horrible day, and food is your addiction, then you might eat a whole bag of Oreos. You feel full afterward, and maybe your sad feelings go away for a minute. But that double-stuffed treat won't help your heart. That burst of sugar may make you feel better for a moment, but it's not healthy for your body, and it can't change what's really bothering you deep down inside. Once you finish all those Oreos, you'll probably end up feeling guilty— and have a bellyache!

THINK ABOUT IT

Addictions can be big or small. What addictions do you see in your own life? What are the things you turn to that make you feel better—at least for a little while? How are those addictions hurting you?

_____

_____

_____

_____

_____

We need to look past the thing we're addicted to and figure out *why* we're addicted to it. Where is the pain coming from? Until we figure that out, the giant of addiction is not going to fall.

Fortunately, there is an answer: Christ.

JESUS TAKES DOWN THE GIANT OF OUR ADDICTIONS.

Jesus takes down the giant of our addictions. Because we live in a sinful world, there will always be times when we feel weak and vulnerable. We will still want to hide and cover it up. But instead of running to our addiction, the answer is to run to Jesus.

Let's look at David's life to see how this works.

ARMOR THAT DOESN'T FIT

When David got ready to head off to battle Goliath, King Saul told David exactly what he thought:

"You are not able." (1 Samuel 17:33)

Then Saul went on to explain why: "You are only a young man, and he has been a warrior from his youth" (v. 33).

At first, it sounds like King Saul was worried about David. But I think Saul was trying to make David feel vulnerable. King Saul was a big, strong, experienced warrior. He was a head taller than any other man in the Israelite army. He had a suit of the best armor. He had a whole army of fighting men at his side. King Saul should have been the one to go out and fight Goliath. But he didn't. Whenever Goliath taunted, King Saul stayed in his tent, worrying. So when this teenage kid, David, came up and declared that he was going to fight the giant, Saul's first reaction was to point out to everybody how difficult it was going to be. How impossible. What Saul really wanted was to save face.

Yet David was respectful. He reminded everyone that he was Saul's servant. David wasn't trying to show up the king. He actually had good reasons for believing he could fight the giant. David said,

> "Your Majesty, I take care of my father's sheep. And when one of them is dragged off by a lion or a bear, I go after it and beat the wild animal until it lets the sheep go. If the wild animal turns and attacks me, I grab it by the throat and kill it.
>
> Sir, I have killed lions and bears that way, and I can kill this worthless Philistine. He shouldn't have made fun of the army of the living God! The LORD has rescued me from the claws of lions and bears, and

he will keep me safe from the hands of this Philistine."
(vv. 34–37 CEV)

Unfortunately, Saul didn't completely trust God like David did. So he dressed David in his own armor. But David wasn't used to all that equipment. He could barely move. Saul wanted David to suit up so David would look stronger and more protected than he really was.

We do the same thing. We try to put on false armor all the time. We feel powerless and afraid. So we wrap ourselves in things—addictions—that promise to make us feel stronger or more protected. But David put aside the armor that weighed him down, and he turned to the Lord. He went out to fight the giant with just himself, his sling, his rod, and his God. That's the example we need to follow.

God wants us to understand that our vulnerability isn't the worst thing in the world. In fact, one of the beautiful things about the word *vulnerable* is that right within the middle of the word we see this promise:

Vulner**ABLE**

With God, we are able. We are able because God is able. And thanks to God, we are not weak—we are strong.

WE
ARE
ABLE
BECAUSE
GOD
IS
ABLE.

THREE STEPS TO STRENGTH

---

1. Turn to Jesus.

When we're feeling vulnerable, we actually have a big opportunity to run to Jesus. We can come to Him just as we are. No hiding. No pretending to be something we're not. Jesus knows and loves us. He calls us His beloved sons and daughters. In Jesus, we are safe. Don't try to cover up your fears or weaknesses. Tell Him about them. Don't turn to some addiction to feel better—it will only end up hurting you. Turn to Jesus.

TELL JESUS ABOUT YOUR FEARS OR WEAKNESSES.

What does turning to Jesus look like in real life? It's going to Jesus in prayer and saying, "I'm having a hard time right now. I'm feeling like I could be attacked any second. Jesus, I am weak, but You are strong. Jesus, with Your help, I can beat this." Jesus blesses this kind of honesty. He doesn't push us away. He pulls us closer to Him, wraps us in His love, and fills us with His strength. When we are vulnerable, Jesus is *ABLE*.

2. Don't fight alone.

When we're battling the giant of addition, the biggest lie we'll face is that we need to fight the battle on our own. Because we're ashamed or afraid, we try to fight in secret. We don't want anyone to know. But the giant goes down when we're honest with God and those around us.

Have you ever felt something powerful in your heart and promised God everything would change? And you did for a while. You stopped hanging out with the wrong crowd. You stopped saying those words and watching that stuff. You stopped whatever it was that was harming you. And you just knew you had this addiction beat. But then, so quickly, you got sucked right back in again.

"What happened?" you ask. "I thought this giant was *dead*!"

Because of Christ, the giant *is* dead. But there's still a battle—and you can't fight it on your own. You

> FREEDOM HAPPENS IN THE LIGHT.

can't hide it. You can't fight this battle by yourself in the dark.

Freedom happens in the light. Bring your struggles into the light of Jesus' grace by telling Him all about them. Then understand that He may use other people to help you. That might mean asking a group of trusted friends to help you avoid the wrong crowd. It might mean talking to your parents and getting their help. Or it might mean reaching out to a trusted teacher, pastor, or youth leader. We all need someone who is willing to tell us when we're headed in the wrong direction and point us back to Jesus again.

3. When you are weak, then you are strong.

Huh? When I'm weak, then *I'm strong? What does that even mean?* Let's check out what Paul said in 2 Corinthians 12:7–10:

> To keep me from becoming proud, I was given a thorn
> in my flesh, a messenger from Satan to torment me
> and keep me from becoming proud.
>
> Three different times I begged the Lord to take it
> away. Each time he said, "My grace is all you need.
> My power works best in weakness." So now I am glad
> to boast about my weaknesses, so that the power of
> Christ can work through me. That's why I take pleas-
> ure in my weaknesses, and in the insults, hardships,
> persecutions, and troubles that I suffer for Christ. For
> when I am weak, then I am strong. (NLT)

Here's the picture. Paul was able to do some amazing things for Christ. But to keep him from becoming too proud, God allowed "a thorn" in his flesh. Was it an illness? Was it blindness? Was it somebody dogging him the whole time? Nobody knows exactly what it was. But we know it was something he had to battle and that God allowed it to be there.

You're like, *Okay. You just lost me. Why would God put a thorn in anybody's flesh? Isn't God's plan to bless me and not to curse me, to give me a future and a hope, like Jeremiah 29:11 says?* Yes, it is. When God allowed the thorn in Paul's flesh, He wasn't trying to hurt Paul. God wanted to make Paul stronger. The "thorn" forced Paul to lean on God's strength—which was actually much greater than his own. If Paul hadn't had the thorn, he probably wouldn't have leaned on God as much. That's what Jesus meant when He said to Paul, "My power works best in weakness."

WEAKNESS CAN BE OUR FRIEND. IT MAKES US TURN TO GOD.

That's an example of how weakness can be our friend. It makes us turn to God. That's why Paul said, "So now I am glad to boast about my weaknesses." Everyone who has ever done something great for God had some sort of weakness.

- Jacob wrestled with God and limped the rest of his life. Yet Jacob became the father of the twelve tribes of Israel.

- Moses was not an eloquent speaker, and he was afraid to talk to Pharaoh. He asked God to choose someone else instead. Yet God used Moses to confront Pharaoh and lead His people out of Egypt.
- Peter denied Christ three times because he was afraid. Yet Jesus gave Peter the boldness to start His church.
- John was thrown into exile on the island of Patmos where he was likely a slave in a rock quarry. Yet Jesus gave him glimpses of heaven, and he wrote the book of Revelation.
- Jesus' head was pierced with a thorny crown. He was spat on, whipped, and crucified on a cross between two thieves. Yet God the Father raised Him up from death to life. His blood set us free from sin.

Why does God allow thorns in our lives? It's not to hurt us. Rather, it is to help us remember to turn to Him so that we can experience even more of His power.

Do you want to be strong? Do you want to be a stronger student, a stronger son or daughter, a stronger friend, a stronger leader? Then admit your weakness. Let Jesus accept you just as you are, and He will exchange your weakness for His strength. Then accept His invitation to do things you couldn't do on your own.

JESUS
WILL
EXCHANGE
YOUR
WEAKNESS
FOR
HIS
STRENGTH.

YOUR WEAKNESS, GOD'S STRENGTH

Is Jesus inviting you to do something you couldn't do on your own? Write it here.

_____

Is there something holding you back? Name it here.

_____

Ask Jesus to take your weakness and fill you with His strength instead. Write your prayer here.

_____

_____

_____

_____

_____

CHAPTER 8

A Table for Two

When we read the story of David and Goliath and try to apply it to our lives, we have to remember the twist I mentioned earlier in the book—we aren't David in the story. Jesus is.

Goliath was taken down by a shepherd, which is interesting because Jesus calls Himself our Shepherd many times in the Bible. And He promises to lead, guide, and protect us—*in the presence of our enemies*. While we're praying something like, "God, get me away from this giant," God is keeping us there, but He is sending a Shepherd to save us right smack in the middle of the fight.

That Shepherd is best described in David's own words from Psalm 23.

The LORD is my shepherd, I lack nothing.

He makes me lie down in green pastures,
he leads me beside quiet waters,

he refreshes my soul.
He guides me along the right paths

for his name's sake.
Even though I walk

through the darkest valley,
I will fear no evil,

for you are with me;
your rod and your staff,

they comfort me.
You prepare a table before me

in the presence of my enemies.
You anoint my head with oil;

my cup overflows.
Surely your goodness and love will follow me

all the days of my life,
and I will dwell in the house of the LORD

forever.

Most of us would like that psalm to read, "He prepares a table before me in *His* presence"—a table far away from the battle and the giants. But God doesn't promise to instantly save us from trouble. What He promises is something even more amazing and powerful. Right in the middle of the battle, with all the giants standing around, our Shepherd spreads out a feast for us with everything we need. It's a table for two. One seat for you and one seat for the God who is for you.

SET A TABLE

Sometimes a truth becomes even more powerful when we see it with our own eyes. So set a table for two—for you and Jesus. It can be an actual table, a cardboard box, a picnic blanket, or just a spot on the floor. Set out two plates and cups and napkins. Add a snack, if you'd like. And then spread out the feast—your Bible. Thank God for coming, and ask Him to give you what you need today. And then feast on His Word.

THE PARTY CRASHER

But then there's Satan. He's described in 1 Peter 5 as an enemy who "prowls around like a roaring lion looking for someone to devour" (v. 8). Of course, Satan isn't actually a lion; he just roars like one to scare you.

Jesus is *the* Lion—the Lion of Judah. His roar shatters the Enemy. He defeated Satan when He died on the cross and was raised to life again. But even though Satan has already lost, he keeps on fighting—and he won't stop until Jesus comes back again one day. In the meantime, Satan prowls around looking for a way to sneak into your life. If you don't stop him, he'll crash the party and pull up a chair at your table.

JESUS IS *THE* LION—THE LION OF JUDAH. HIS ROAR SHATTERS THE ENEMY.

Of course, he won't look like the Enemy. He'll disguise himself as someone helpful or something to make you feel better. With a big smile, the Enemy will stroll right up to you, and before you know it, you're having a conversation with a killer. The first thing he'll probably tell you is that God's not good and you can't trust Him. Because that's what Satan has been saying since day one in the garden of Eden. And if that doesn't work, he'll whip out this dagger—*If God is so good, then why do you have all these troubles and all this pain in your life?*

That question is hard to fight because we all feel pain. And there is no "big" or "little" pain when you're hurting. There's just pain. When we're hurting, it's all too easy to believe the Enemy's lies.

But here's how we fight him. We believe what we read in the Bible:

- God is good (Psalm 107:1).
- God has everything under control (Proverbs 19:21).
- In everything God works for the good of His followers (Romans 8:28).
- One day there will be no sadness or tears (Revelation 21:4).
- One day all the wrongs will be made right (Psalm 33:5).

Even though we know all those things, when we're hurting, we struggle to believe that God really is on our side, walking through the dark valley with us. We know the truth, but we can't seem to believe that the truth really will set us free.

So what do we do?

PUTTING THE PIECES TOGETHER

In this chapter, I want to put all the pieces together for us. Some sort of giant is taunting us. Some sort of pain is in our lives. Some sort of trouble is stealing God's glory in our lives and keeping us from living the rich lives God wants us to live.

So how do we make sure that our giants will actually fall?

Don't give the Enemy a seat at your table.

God has prepared a great table for *you*. Not for Satan. But he may have already slipped in and pulled up a chair. How can you know? Look for one of his four favorite lies.

THE FOUR LIES OF THE ENEMY

Lie #1: You're not going to make it.

Remember, according to Psalm 23, the table is in the middle of your enemies. So the Devil can quickly spin your head around and show you that you're surrounded by giants on every side. He whispers, *You're not going to make it. You'll never win this fight. Just quit believing all this "my giant is dead" nonsense and give up. You're done.*

But also remember that the table is set for two. Jesus the Shepherd is there with you. Let Him speak to you. Lock onto His words and let them sink in. David wrote, "Even though I walk *through* the darkest valley" (Psalm 23:4, emphasis added). David knew he wasn't stuck in that valley. He knew his Shepherd would lead him through to the other side. There would be green pastures, quiet water, and rest for his soul on the other side.

And until then, there was a table filled with everything he needed in the middle of the fight.

Don't give the Enemy a seat at your table. You *are* going to make it.

Lie #2: There's something better at another table.

The Enemy also tempts you with thoughts like these:

Look over there.

Hey, the party's at that other table. It's way more fun over there.

Your table is lame.

Being at a different table is definitely going to make you feel better.

God left you in the dark valley. Forget Him and just go do whatever you want!

Satan is not just out to get you; he's out to steal God's glory too. You see, you were created in the image of God with extraordinary purpose and promise. You are God's prized possession. If Satan can slash your heart, he can break the heart of God.

Don't listen to his lies. There's nothing better than Jesus. No party. No seat at the popular kids' table. No grade. No spot on the team. Jesus wants the very best for you, and He will never keep from you what is truly good.

If you're at the table with Jesus, then you've got the best seat in the house.

Lie #3: You're not good enough for God.

The Enemy also likes to whisper things like these:

You don't matter.

You've never mattered to anyone.

God doesn't care about you.

You don't deserve a table with God.

God doesn't love you anymore. In fact, He never loved you in the first place.

You are too far away from God. God's finished with you. There is no way back.

When Psalm 23 was written, the word *table* meant "feast." Only important people were able to afford throwing a feast. And important people would only invite other important people to their table. So when God prepares a table for you—guess what! That means *you're* important to Him. He puts out the very best of everything you need—for your heart, soul, mind, and body—to survive the battle. And He invites you to dine with Him. He invites you because He cares for you. He invites you because He has already given everything for you. He has already given you Jesus.

Jesus gives us a similar promise in John 10:11: "I am the good shepherd. The good shepherd lays down his life for the sheep." The Enemy will tell you that you don't matter and that no one cares about you. But all it takes is one look at the cross to know that's a lie.

Don't give the Enemy a seat at your table. You are treasured by the God of the universe.

Lie #4: Everyone is out to get you.

Okay, maybe there is someone in your family or school or even at church who is actually saying bad things about you. But when you start thinking that *everyone* is out to get you, that's when Satan has pulled up at chair at your table.

Have you had the Enemy tell you things like these?

No one likes you.

Everyone is against you.

Everybody is talking bad about you.

They are all plotting against you.

You better watch your back.

That kind of thinking doesn't come from the good Shepherd but from the Enemy at our table.

Even if everyone is against us (though it's usually only a handful of people), Christ's table gives us all we need to make it through. Don't focus on the giants. Focus on the fact that Jesus is sitting with you. His presence at our table is greater than the presence of any enemy around us.

God's got your back—and your front, sides, top, and bottom (Psalm 139:5).

Don't give the Enemy a seat at your table.

DON'T
GIVE
THE
ENEMY
A
SEAT
AT
YOUR
TABLE.

HOW GIANTS FALL

—

Giants don't just fall over on their own. And no matter how big or strong or brave you are, you can't knock them down by yourself. You need Jesus. He's the only One who can knock down your giants. So check out these six ways to bring the power of Jesus into your battles.

1. Make sure Jesus is in your life.

We need to make sure we really have Jesus in our lives. It's as simple as that. John lays it out for us like this: "Whoever has the Son has life; whoever does not have the Son of God does not have life" (1 John 5:12). Is Jesus in your life? Is Jesus *your* Shepherd? If not, why not decide to follow Jesus right here, right now, today?

When we follow Jesus, we realize that our sins are separating us from God. But the good news is that Jesus Christ came to earth. He was born as a baby in Bethlehem. He lived on earth for thirty-three years. He was crucified. He died. He was buried in a borrowed tomb. And then Jesus was raised to life again. All so we can have a relationship with God—on earth and forever in heaven. God loves the world so much that He gave His only Son to us. Whoever believes in Jesus will not die but have eternal life (John 3:16).

You may be wondering, *But what do I have to do to be saved?* The answer is simple: "Believe in the Lord Jesus, and you will be saved" (Acts 16:31). It's that simple. But this is more than simply believing that Jesus is real. It's trusting, following, and obeying Him. Because when you do those three things—trust, follow, and obey—you open up your life for all the power of Jesus to flow in.

Do you want the giants in your life to fall? Trusting Jesus as your Savior and Lord is the first step in the fight. That's how the giants go down.

Have you done that? If not, do it right now. Pray this prayer with me:

"Lord Jesus, God Almighty, please
save me from my sins.
I don't want to be separated from You anymore.
I believe that You gave Your life on
the cross to pay for my sins.
I believe that You rose in victory from the grave.
Please forgive me for all my sins.
Wash all the guilt and shame away.
Jesus, make me alive in You.
I accept You as my Savior and Lord.
And I want to follow You all the days of my life.
Thank You for finding me and saving me.
I believe it. I receive it.
Amen."

If you prayed this prayer, share your good news with someone you trust, like your parents, siblings, or pastor.

2. Let Jesus lead you day by day.

We all like to think we're pretty good at being our own boss. We don't exactly love it when others try to tell us what to do—even if it means our lives will be better. Even allowing God to lead us can be a struggle.

But freedom from our giants begins when we humble ourselves before God. That means we go to Him and admit we need His help—every day. We listen for His voice and ask Him to guide us through the valley to the other side.

Some years ago my friend Marc and I set out to climb the Matterhorn, one of the tallest and most famous mountains in the world. We didn't know much about mountain climbing. And we didn't know that the mountain we picked was one of the deadliest climbs out there. So we arrived in the little village of Zermatt, Switzerland, full of confidence. Secretly, I knew I had *not* crushed our training program. But since I'm pretty athletic, I didn't worry. That is, until I came face-to-face with the mountain. *How,* I thought, *are we possibly going to get up that thing?*

After a week of training, the Swiss mountain guides cleared us to make the climb. I was still worried, but our training guide kept saying, "Don't worry. It's a 'walk up.' We'll go super slow, and all you need to do is put one foot in front of the other."

That's what a life with Jesus is—a "walk up." It's believing *each day* that He will lead us, and then we follow His lead. We won't jump right to the top of our faith any more than I jumped right to the top of the mountain. We put one foot in front of the other, day after day.

3. Trust Jesus.

We've already talked about depending on Jesus to slay the giants for us. Our responsibility is to trust Him through the battle. That means we follow Him. We pray that the giants will fall in Jesus' name, and then we act like they already have.

You are a work in progress. And Jesus will keep working on you until the day He makes you perfect and takes you home to heaven with Him. Sometimes that work will be uncomfortable. Keep praying. Keep trusting. If you need to, talk to a counselor, a parent, or a trusted friend or group of friends. Or maybe you grab a journal and work it out—just you and Jesus. Or maybe there's a health issue that's making the problem worse, and you need to see a doctor. There's nothing wrong with using all the tools Jesus gives you.

Giants fall in different ways for different people as we keep walking with Christ.

ONE STEP AT A TIME

The thing about following Jesus is that He doesn't usually show you exactly where you're going or how you're going to get there. It's like when God asked Abraham to leave his home and said, "Go to the land that I will show you" (Genesis 12:1 CEV). Like Abraham, you just have to keep following Him, one step at a time, doing the next right thing and then the next right thing. But in Matthew 28:20, Jesus gives us a promise that makes the journey not only possible but also amazing. It's a promise you'll find throughout the Bible in verses like Isaiah 41:10 and Deuteronomy 31:6. Look them up for yourself. What is the promise? What does it mean for your walk with Jesus?

_____

_____

_____

_____

_____

4. Say yes to the Holy Spirit.

The Holy Spirit is the third person of the Trinity—God the Father, Son, and Holy Spirit. He is Christ's gift to us, the Spirit and power of Christ who comes to live inside us. The Spirit speaks to our hearts and nudges us in the right direction. The more we listen to Him and follow Him, the more we will hear His voice.

Back to the Matterhorn . . .

Marc and I spent the night high on the mountain after a grueling hike the day before. We walked out of our hut before dawn the next day and were immediately secured to our guides with 120 feet of rope. Then we stepped into the cold, dark morning for the 4,300-foot climb to the top. In my head I comforted myself by repeating what my training guide had told me: *It's a "walk up." We'll go super slow, and all you need to do is put one foot in front of the other.* But about five minutes in, that comfort vanished as we ran into a fifty-foot wall of rock with a fixed rope hanging down. The wall went straight up like the side of a building. My guide, Richard (who was *not* the guy I had trained with), disappeared into the darkness. Before I lost sight of him, he said, "I'll go up and get secure. When you feel me tug on the rope, climb behind me."

What? When you get where? Climb on what?

A minute or two later a little jolt hit my harness. So I grabbed the rope and started hauling myself up. We were so high up that the oxygen was thin, so every breath was work. I pulled with all my might.

This happened several times over the next four hours. We'd get to a hard spot in the climb. Richard would vanish. I'd feel the tug on my harness. I'd get moving. Soon we'd meet back up and repeat.

Here's the point: You may be facing a fifty-foot wall you have no idea how to climb, but that's okay. Your Shepherd will do the leading. He's ahead of you right now. He's secure and ready to support you if you should slip. He gives you a tug to start climbing. You take a step. You might be shocked that you can take that step, since the Enemy keeps telling you that you can't. But you are linked to Jesus and constantly led by His Spirit.

When the tug from the Spirit comes, say yes. Again and again. You'll be amazed at what you can climb.

5. Don't take no for an answer.

Let's be honest: some of us *like* our giants. They've been in our lives for so long that we're comfortable with them. We know the giants need to go, but there's security in having those giants there. Sure, they're harmful, but they're also familiar. We tend to stick with the things we know even when they aren't good for us. And to make it worse, the Enemy says, *No,*

DON'T TAKE NO FOR AN ANSWER.

GOLIATH MUST FALL FOR YOUNG READERS

this giant won't fall. No, it can't be done. No, you can't win the victory.

Don't take no for an answer.

Sitting at the table with Jesus is a safe place, but it's not always a comfortable place. That's because when we want our giants to fall, we have to follow Jesus with all our hearts. And the Enemy is not going to like that.

You have to think: *I've got to get rid of this giant. This thing isn't some cute, cuddly little pet anymore. This thing is trouble. It's a killer. I've got to get rid of it now!*

Yes, the battle is won, but we are still in a fight. We've got to move forward and get rid of that giant. Trust Jesus to do what only He can do.

6. Keep your guard up.

There are giants all throughout the land. It was true for David. (Did you know Goliath had brothers?) And it's true for us. But we don't need to be afraid. We just need to stay alert.

When the giants of fear or anger or addiction leave our lives, they can leave an empty space behind. We need to be sure we fill that empty space with Jesus.

Even when we stick close to Christ, giants can still throw rocks at us. Remember, Jesus never promises us a problem-free life. Yes, there is still the valley of the shadow of death, and yes, there are still giants roaming

164

JESUS WILL LEAD US **THROUGH** THAT DARK VALLEY.

around. But Jesus leads us through the valley. Jesus prepares a table for us—with everything we need—right in front of our enemies.

When a giant attacks, we might wonder why bad things keep happening to us. We might even wonder if God still loves us. All we have to do is look at the cross to know the answer. *That's* how much God loves us. And He asks us to trust Him in both good times and tough times. Remember everything that was thrown at Jesus? The mocking? The laughter? The beatings? The crucifixion? Jesus knows all about suffering, pain, and loss. He understands everything we're going through. And if we stick close to Him, He'll lead us through that dark valley.

So what does it look like to keep your guard up?

Let's say your giant is acceptance. And you find acceptance by hanging out with the wrong crowd. They encourage you to do, watch, or say things you know are wrong and hurtful. But you go along with it because you want to fit in. As Jesus works in your life and you find your acceptance in Him, that giant will eventually fall. But there will likely still be days when you feel lonely or rejected. And you'll be tempted to run back to that crowd. Run to Jesus instead. Ask Him to bring new friends into your life. Ask Him to replace the bad with good. And in the meantime, read the promises of Psalm 23. Take a seat at that table He has for you. Or head outside for a walk and a talk with Jesus. Tell Him how you feel, give your worries to Him, and let His Holy Spirit comfort your heart and mind.

Your giant is dead, but just like those snake bodies, it might wriggle from time to time. And you might slip up. You might find yourself hanging out with that giant again. If that happens, that doesn't mean you've lost. Just tell Jesus; ask Him to forgive you and help you. And then accept His grace. When you turn back to God, He will always forgive you. *Always*.

KEEP YOUR GUARD UP

What giant are you facing today? And what action can you take to prepare for the next time you'll face it? You could stop to pray. You could recite a Bible verse about God's power. Or you could reach out to a friend and share what you're going through.

Write down your plan for keeping your guard up.

_____

_____

_____

COME TO THE TABLE

Let me close this chapter by inviting you to sit with Jesus at a table for two. I want to give you a challenge: dive into Psalm 23. Soak up the words and plant them in your heart. How? Well, Goliath taunted the Israelites for forty days and forty nights. So let's throw a stone of truth at your giants by reading Psalm 23 every morning and evening for forty days. You can read it in a Bible or listen to it on an app. Make it the first and last thing you do every day.

Before you go to sleep, say, "Tell me, Lord Jesus, about who You are, about where You are leading me, and about what my future is. Show me Your goodness." When you wake up in the morning, say, "Tell me again." If you need a break in the middle of the day, say, "Tell me again." If you need some encouragement to keep you going in the middle of the day, say, "Tell me again." As you get ready for bed, say, "Tell me again." If your giant wakes you up in the middle of the night, say, "Tell me again."

For forty mornings and forty evenings, let the Shepherd speak over you:

I am able.

I am here.

I am good.

CHAPTER 9

Fuel for the Fight

If you've been keeping track of the twists and turns in this book, then you'll remember that we started with a couple of big ones: In the story of David and Goliath, we are not David; Jesus is David. And our giant is already dead; Jesus has already won the victory for us.

Now, let's look at one final twist. The reason David went out to fight Goliath was not to win honor for himself. It was to give glory and honor and fame to God.

And that's why we should fight our giants too.

For God's glory.

This is *so* important to understand. Yes, God wants us to be free of our giants. Yes, God wants our giants to fall. But this isn't just about us. There's more to it than that—God also wants the glory that comes from setting us free from our giants. Not because He's vain or greedy for attention or any of those other things we sometimes struggle with. God wants the glory so that other people will look at our lives and say, "Your God is truly God." And then they'll want Him to be their God too.

Our freedom and God's glory are like two sides of the same coin. They can't ever be separated.

TWO SIDES, ONE COIN

Grab a coin—a penny, a dime, a quarter—and take a good look at it. The two sides are different, right? But it's still just the one coin. Your freedom from sin and fear and anger and all those other giants is like one side of a coin. God's glory is the other side. How are they connected? How does your freedom give glory to God?

_____

_____

_____

_____

_____

Back on that battlefield, when David heard Goliath throw out his insults, he could have turned around and headed straight back home again. David's life wasn't in danger. He was just the delivery guy. He could've said, "How tall is that guy? Nine feet tall? He looks mean. I'm out of here. I'm heading back home to Dad. The food is in your tents. See you later." Nobody would have called him a coward. He would've done what a lot of people would have done—ignored the problem and walked away.

Yet that's not what David did.

Why?

David went out to fight Goliath because this giant was cursing the God of Israel. David said, "Oh, whoa. Wait a minute, Goliath. All that stuff you're saying about my God? I'm not putting up with that today. You're going to stop taunting my God, right here and now. And you're going down. In fact, you *must* go down because God's glory is what we're all about."

Even what Jesus did on the cross was to give God glory. Jesus gave His life to say, "See this? You're about to be a part of something amazing right here. All the stuff that's holding you back from being everything God created you to be—your sins, your fears, your giants? I'm giving you a way out of all that. I'm setting you free. And I'm doing it so that people will know that the God of Israel is the one true God. He is the God of mercy,

OUR
PURPOSE
IN LIFE IS
TO ENJOY
THIS
GREAT
GOD
AND
GIVE HIM
GLORY
FOREVER.

kindness, grace, compassion, and love. He is the God who doesn't hold our sins against us—He sacrificed His own Son instead. He is the only One who can do that. Because He is the only true God!"

One of the greatest temptations we face is to make our relationship with Jesus all about us. We turn Jesus into a self-help trick, saying, "He helps me feel better." But it's not all about us. We are not His maker; He is our Maker. Our purpose in life is to enjoy this great God *and* give Him glory forever.

One of the ways we give God glory is by letting Him knock down our giants. Not just because it helps us, but also because it helps us show the world who Jesus is and how powerful He is.

MADE TO GIVE GLORY

———

When God made each of us, He had a plan. We were designed to depend on our Creator and to shine His greatness and glory into the world. God gives us life and breath and blessings and opportunities, and then God gets the credit and glory and praise from our lives.

This is what we are made for. God's glory.

Think of it this way: if you're on a sports team or

in a club, you know what it means to wear the uniform so that everyone knows you're a part of that team. In the same way, when we praise and give glory to God, we do it not only to let people know we're a part of God's team but also to share how amazing He is.

So what does glory really look like?

BLUE GLORY

I was raised on Auburn University football. My earliest memories of college football are of listening to Auburn games on the radio and watching my dad yell into the speakers as if everyone at the game could hear him. When Auburn made a game-winning play, you would find my dad, my sister, and me dancing on the sofa and the coffee table, screaming our heads off.

After my dad died, I took my mom to an Auburn game as a special way to remember Dad. We arrived on campus in the pouring-down rain. (And when I say it was pouring rain, think Noah's flood. I may have seen an elephant floating by.) We ended up buying trash bags at the local supermarket, cutting holes in them, and wearing them like ponchos.

You'd think no one would show up in that kind of

weather, but you'd be wrong. We were playing against the number-one-ranked team, so close to eighty thousand of us packed into that stadium. The cheerleaders started a chant. On the opposite side of the stadium, they held up signs toward the crowd, which was followed by a loud and determined shout—*O R A N G E!*

Quickly our side shouted back—*B L U E!*

And so it began, with each shout getting louder than the one before.

O R A N G E!

B L U E!

At one point I looked over at my sixty-five-year-old mom. Her hair was plastered to her head as if she were standing in the shower. The veins were sticking out on the side of her neck. Then, as if she were going to single-handedly drown out the forty thousand people across from us, she took a huge breath. Her eyes were bulging as she screamed—a deep, rattling, scary scream—

B L U U U U U U U U U U U U U U U E!

Man!

There we were, in a driving rain, yelling like we'd been set on fire. Why? So we could cheer for *two colors.*

That, my friends, is glory. Not heavenly glory, mind you. But glory for sure.

What would it be like to live that way for God's fame and glory?

A BAD DAY FOR DAGON

In the Old Testament the ark of the covenant was the most treasured possession of God's people. It represented God's very presence and glory among them. You can check out the whole story in these three passages: 1 Samuel 4:1–7:1, 2 Samuel 6, and 1 Chronicles 15–16.

Once again the Israelites were in battle with the Philistines, although this wasn't the fight with Goliath. And once again, the battle wasn't going well for the Israelites. So the priests brought the ark of the covenant down to the battlefield as if to say, "Hey, now we have the holy ark of the Lord, and we can't be beat."

When the ark came down, the Israelites let loose with this huge roar, and the Philistines were like, "Uh-oh. We've heard about this ark. We're doomed. It's the same God who struck the Egyptians with all kinds of plagues in the wilderness. Be strong, Philistines! Be men and fight!"

But there was a problem. God wasn't in on the plan, because the hearts of the Israelites who called for the ark were wicked. God let the Philistines win that day. They even stole the ark and carted it back to their city of Ashdod. There, they placed it in the temple of their god, Dagon, a tall, stone idol. They did this to taunt the Israelites. It was a way of saying, "Ha-ha. There you are, nice little shiny ark of the covenant. You sit right there with Dagon. Dagon is amazing."

Here's what happened. The Philistines all went home to party that night after thinking they'd showed the Israelites whose god was who. But when they came back the next morning, their god had fallen over facedown in front of the ark of the covenant of God. *How'd that happen?* None of the Philistines could figure it out. So they spent a day propping Dagon back up. Once that was done, they went off to party again. The next morning, same thing. Dagon was on the ground again, lying flat before the ark of God. This time Dagon's head and hands were broken off. To add to the insult, the head and the hands were piled up in the doorway. The Philistines had to step over their broken-down god to get into the temple.

You know why the Philistines' god was knocked down? Because God is serious about His glory. And when there was nobody to defend His glory, God defended it Himself. Don't you love that? God was like, *Oh, so you're going to put Me in here with that piece of stone? I will crush your tiny god into pea gravel. You can put him in the bottom of your aquarium. Oh, you're propping up your god again after I pushed him over? No problem, Philistines. I'll take this as far as*

GOD IS SERIOUS ABOUT HIS GLORY.

you want to go. I am God—period. I will not give My glory to another god or share any of My praise with false idols. I won't sit here and be taunted by a rock. I don't care how tall the statue of your Dagon is; it must go down.

Finally, the Philistines clued in and returned the ark of God to Israel.

Sadly, the Israelites forgot how to properly carry the ark, and lives were lost. After several failed attempts, King David finally had the ark brought to Jerusalem on poles—which was what God had said to do in the first place!

As the ark journeyed toward the city, David and his men were so grateful to be in the presence of such glory that they took six steps, then built an altar and offered a sacrifice of praise to God! Then they took another six steps, built another altar, and offered another sacrifice of praise to God. Over and over again, that's how they moved—in constant worship—all the way to Jerusalem.

David had a heart that longed for God's glory—even more than he wanted his own glory. Remember what David said to Goliath just before Goliath went down:

"You come against me with sword and spear and javelin, but I come against you in the name of the LORD Almighty, the God of the armies of Israel, whom you have defied. This day the LORD will deliver you into my hands, and I'll strike you down and cut off your head. This very day I will give the carcasses of the Philistine army to the birds and the wild animals, and the whole world will know that there is a God in Israel. All those gathered here will know that it is not by sword or spear that the LORD saves; for the battle is the LORD's, and he will give all of you into our hands." (1 Samuel 17:45–47)

The first thing David said to Goliath was, "Hey, Goliath, you're going down. Today." Then David looked up at all the Philistine soldiers on the hillside and said, "And all the rest of you are going down with him!" Then David told them why: "You're going down so the whole world will know that there is a God in Israel. Everyone here will know that this battle is the Lord's, and He will give all of you into our hands."

We know the rest of the story. David took his sling and with one rock silenced the giant.

THIS BATTLE IS THE LORD'S.

David was a shepherd boy who fell in love with the God of wonders beyond our galaxy. He was the teen who faced down the dreaded Philistine giant. And he was the man after God's own heart. But David would have understood the scene in the stadium with my mom and me in the pouring-down rain. Because David was known to get a bit crazy himself when it came to giving glory to God. When the ark of the covenant was at last returned to Jerusalem, David threw off his kingly robes and danced with all his might as the ark was carried into the city—wearing only a thin piece of linen! When his wife accused him of not acting like a king, David declared he would do even crazier things than that to give glory to God.

THE BEST WAY TO GIVE GLORY TO GOD IS ACTUALLY PRETTY SIMPLE: OBEY HIM.

But giving glory to God doesn't have to mean something crazy like dancing through the city streets in your undies. The best way to give glory to God is actually pretty simple: obey Him. When you say no to your giant of acceptance and refuse to watch that R-rated movie your friends are pressuring you to watch, you give glory to God. When you forgive that person who hurt you and leave the giant of anger in the dust, you give glory to God. And when you decide to ignore the giant of fear and stick up for that kid everyone else is laughing at, you give glory to God.

Giving glory to God is what you were created to do. And our God gives us so many reasons to praise Him.

THINK ABOUT IT

So what would it look like to give God glory in your life? Here are some ideas:

- Be like David and dance to a praise song while you sing about how great God is.
- Write your own song of praise.
- Find a way, at least once every day, to tell someone how awesome God is.
- Give God the credit—for beautiful weather, for the wonders of His creation, for the good things that happen in your life.
- And when not-so-good things happen in your life, declare that you know God will still take care of you.

What are other ways you can give glory to God?

_____

_____

_____

_____

_____

FROM MESS TO MASTERPIECE

We have all messed up. We have all sinned. Our choices have disappointed ourselves and those around us. But God is able to take the messy mistakes of our lives and turn them into something beautiful that brings Him praise.

As we look across our own Valley of Elah, we see our giants taunting us and seeking to steal God's glory. But we have a champion in our story, and He is sitting with us right now as we come to the end of this book. His name is Jesus, and He takes down giants and gives freedom to us all.

I don't want you to close this book and think Jesus is asking you to try harder. No, He's not asking you to fight these battles on your own. He is simply asking you to see Him—to see the work He has already done for you and to believe that He can make a masterpiece from any mess.

Jesus is inviting you to focus on Him and to rest in His grace. Follow Him—right this moment—with your very next step. And keep on doing that step after step. If you do, He will bless you with your freedom and His glory.

Goliath must fall. *Your* Goliath must fall—because Jesus has already knocked that giant down.

So live like it has fallen. Live like Jesus is fighting your giants for you, because He is. And live like Jesus has won, because He has.

JESUS
HAS
ALREADY
KNOCKED
THAT
GIANT
DOWN.

IT'S TIME FOR YOUR GIANTS TO FALL

What giant is taunting you? Maybe it's more than one. Name your giant—or giants—here.

_____

_____

Now, flip back through the pages of this book. What truths will make that giant fall? Make a list of them here.

_____

_____

_____

If your giants start to get a little too noisy—because they still like to yell and shout, even though they've been crushed—look back over this list. Remind yourself of who fights for you. And tell that giant, "My God is bigger than you!"

The Story Isn't Over: The Armor of God

You made it!

You've figured out what your giants are, how they attack you, and how you can live with the assurance that they've already been defeated—because Jesus has already knocked those giants down.

So what do you do now? The truth is, your giants may still come around, and your story is far from over. You need a way to defend yourself.

Well, the best way to prepare for battle is by putting on the armor of God. Take a look at Ephesians 6:10–18:

Finally, be strong in the Lord and in his mighty power. Put on the full armor of God, so that you can take your stand against the devil's schemes. For our struggle is not against flesh and blood, but against the rulers, against the authorities, against the powers of this dark world and against the spiritual forces of evil in the heavenly realms. Therefore put on the full armor of God, so that when the day of evil comes, you may be able to stand your ground, and after you have done everything, to stand. Stand firm then, with the belt of truth buckled around your waist, with the breastplate of righteousness in place, and with your feet fitted with the readiness that comes from the gospel of peace. In addition to all this, take up the shield of faith, with which you can extinguish all the flaming arrows of the evil one. Take the helmet of salvation and the sword of the Spirit, which is the word of God.

And pray in the Spirit on all occasions with all kinds of prayers and requests. With this in mind, be alert and always keep on praying for all the Lord's people.

Now, you may be thinking, *That sounds nice and all, but how do I really put on the armor of God?* It's not as hard as you might think if you break it down.

Belt of truth: You put on this belt when you believe what God says. The giants in your life are taunting you and insulting you and telling you not to trust God. But when you wear the belt of truth, you say, "What God says is true. And He says that this giant does not have power over me anymore."

Breastplate of righteousness: Making the right decisions can be tough, especially when your friends choose a different path. But when you make decisions based on what God says is right, you're wearing the breastplate of righteousness. And when your decisions are more focused on pleasing God than pleasing yourself or taking the easy way out, your heart is protected.

Shoes fitted with the readiness that comes from the gospel of peace: You only have to trip on your shoelaces once to realize that your shoes, when fitted properly, keep you steady. They give you a firm foundation. And when you're fighting a giant, you need a foundation of peace to prepare for an attack. If you don't feel steady or you're overwhelmed with worry, ask God for peace. He'll give it to you (John 16:33).

Shield of faith: Some days you might feel the giant's spear aimed right at you. But when you ask God to guide and help you when you face something hard, your shield of faith will keep the giant's attacks at arm's length.

Helmet of salvation: If you've given your life to Jesus, you already have the helmet of salvation. (And if you haven't yet but want to, check out the prayer on page 158.) But you can still put on this helmet each day by remembering the hope you have in Christ. Jesus defeated the Enemy. He defeated your giants. You're saved by

God's grace, and one day you'll live in heaven with God. When you hear you giants taunting, ask God to replace those harmful thoughts with His hope instead.

Sword of the Spirit: When your giant attacks, attack back! How? You can do this the same way Jesus fought temptation—by quoting Scripture (Matthew 4:1–11). The sword of the Spirit is the Bible. So use this sword by reading God's Word and memorizing verses that focus on God's power and peace. Check out Philippians 4:13, Isaiah 41:10, and John 16:33. As soon as a giant whispers a harmful thought, recite the verses. Say them out loud if you need to. No giant is a match against the sword of the Spirit.

Once you've put on the full armor of God, it's time to think like a warrior. Stay alert! Keep your eyes peeled, your ears open, and your heart tuned in to God so that if an attack is coming, you'll be ready.

As we close, write a prayer below asking God to help you put on the armor of God and to keep you alert to all your giants' attacks.

_____

_____

_____

_____

About the Author

Louie Giglio is the pastor of Passion City Church and the original visionary of the Passion movement, which exists to call a generation to leverage their lives for the fame of Jesus.

Since 1997, Passion has gathered collegiate-aged people at events across the US and around the world. In 2022, Passion hosted over 50,000 students in the Mercedes-Benz Stadium with another one million people joining online.

Louie is the national-bestselling author of over a dozen books, including *Don't Give the Enemy a Seat at Your Table, At the Table with Jesus, Goliath Must Fall, Indescribable: 100 Devotions About God and Science, The Comeback, The Air I Breathe, I Am Not but I Know I Am*, and others. As a communicator, Louie is widely known for messages such as "Indescribable" and "How Great Is Our God."

An Atlanta native and graduate of Georgia State University, Louie has done postgraduate work at Baylor University and holds a master's degree from Southwestern Baptist Theological Seminary.

Louie and his wife, Shelley, make their home in Atlanta.

Other books from Louie Giglio

Goliath Must Fall

Not Forsaken

The Comeback

The Air I Breathe

I Am Not But I
Know I Am

How Great Is
Our God

Indescribable

The Wonder
of Creation

Indescribable
for Little Ones

Indescribable Activity
Book for Kids

Indescribable
Atlas Adventures